Have I Had Enough?

A glimpse into the mind of an addict,
and his empowering struggle
to find the
faith to surrender;

Awakening the Warrior Within...

Written by Ryan David Hiatt

Inmate # 146884

CONTENTS

A Note from the Author 5

PART I
'THE BATTLE WITHIN'

Broken. 9
Have I Had Enough? 16
The Beginning. 20
The Thunder Rolls. 28
1085 Echo. 35
Like a Dog to his Vomit. 39
Blinded. 43
I'm in Complete Control 49
The Light of Life. 54
Dark Clouds. 58
The Sound of Total Devastation. 63
The Rain Came. 68
Daddy, Where did You Go? 73
The Compromise. 77
The Impending Storm. 82
Secrets and Lies. 88
Hanging by a Moment. 94
Beneath the Bright Lights. 99

PART II
'AWAKENING THE WARRIOR WITHIN'

On a Bus Bound for Prison. 107
I Cannot do This Alone. 112
Be the Man You Want to Be. 116
My Hero. 120
Learning to Stand Tall. 125
Day of Reckoning. 129
Let It Burn. 134
Be Tall, Be Strong, Be True. 139
I've Had Enough. 143

PART III

'STRENGTHENING THE WARRIOR WITHIN'

So, Now What? 148
Watch your Thoughts. 152
Watch your Actions. 164
Watch your Habits. 170
Watch your Character. 173
Have a Little Faith. 177

Epilogue. 182

Notes

Dedicated to:

My son Dominic, I love you buddy.
You are light, you are love, and you are
enough; just the way you are.
I am so proud of you. You are my
inspiration.

To all the children left in the wake of
addiction, may you be blessed with the
hope
and the faith to hold on.

A Note from the Author

Have you ever wondered when enough is enough? Or looked yourself in the mirror and asked, *'Have I Had Enough..?'* Have you ever reached a point where the pain you feel from the choices you've made was almost suffocating? Have you ever felt so trapped, alone, hopeless, or so lost that you just couldn't go on another step?

My name is Ryan; also, known as inmate #146884. I'm currently serving a four-and-a-half-year prison sentence. And, if you've felt that way before, I understand; I've felt that way before too. I have been an addict over fifteen years now. I have lied, stolen, manipulated, and shattered countless hearts while in the clutches of my addiction. I created a swath of chaos, pain, and heartache because of the choices I've made. And, like a vicious hurricane, my addiction spiraled out of control. I've experienced, first hand, the delicate balance of life and death. From drug overdose after drug overdose, lie after lie, guilt upon guilt, shame upon shame.

And for me, I am learning that the battle lines are clearly drawn. The outcome is defined: Life or death. Addiction is not a moral failing, but a disease of the mind; a spiritual malady. The pathway may vary but where it ends always stays the same... Life or death? Joy or pain? Recovery or Relapse? Do I want to go forward or do I want to go back? At times the outcome can be quick and nasty, other times it can be gradual until one day you're compelled to wake up and realize just how much is gone. Either way, one thing is certain: the lines are clearly drawn.

I decided to write this book because I am tired. I'm tired of hurting, inside of me. I am tired of hurting everyone around me. I am tired of feeling guilt, fear, and heart-ache. I am tired of not being authentic. I am tired of not being the man I am designed to be. I wrote this book because *I have had enough*.

In the pages ahead, I have poured my heart, my soul, my truth, and my pain...and I've also shared my hope. May something from my experience reach and touch your heart, and may some of my journey help shine light to you along your path. My prayer is that, in the pages ahead, you may find hope for you and those you love. Thank you for sharing in the journey with me.

With love from your brother and friend,

Ryan

March 29, 2014

Have I Had Enough?

A glimpse into the mind of an addict,
and his empowering struggle
to find the
faith to surrender;

Awakening the Warrior Within.

This is my story...

Part I

'The Battle Within'

"The greatest battle of life is fought within the silent chambers of
your own soul."

-David O. McKay

1

'Broken'

It was the spring of 2003. With the showers of April, it was one of those mornings that seem to just blend together. The rain, misting over the Earth, bringing a cleansing feeling of renewal.

The storm clouds in the sky were barely visible in the darkness. The sun, shielded by the dark of night, inched its way up. The rain continued to fall, washing dirt from the leaves, the rooftops, and down along the concrete floor.

The city was sleeping as the light from the sun remained hidden behind those majestic Rocky Mountains. Each precious second ticked by as the light from the sun neared the mountain peaks...the crest in its daily ritual to light up the darkness. As the sun rose, the rain fell; progressively harder the raindrops pounded the earth.

One drop landed on the leaf of an old tree rooted firmly near the side of the interstate. The drop fell, from one leaf to the next, 'til it finally splashed on the face of the young man's body; curled-up along the side of the interstate.

The young man's body lay cold, stiff, and soaked to the bone. A ghostly complexion of purples mixed with pale blues and whites. Within his seemingly lifeless body, his struggling heart slowed to the faintest of beats. An empty bottle of liquor was clutched firmly in the grasp of his fingertips. With each faint beat of his heart a lethal cocktail of painkillers, cocaine, and alcohol pumped through his veins. The lethal mix was killing him; gradually, viciously, killing him.

His heart somehow continued to beat, but each second proved harder than the last. This battle he so desperately fought within, was nearing its end.

And, one could wonder, what kind of battle this young man was fighting that could have left him for dead on the bank of the interstate that morning? Nevertheless, his organs began shutting down, his toxic blood slowly pooled to the side of his body that lay gripping the embankment...as death kissed his purple lips.

Amidst the looming darkness and death, the sun reached its crest at the mountain peak, casting rays of light and hope on that cold dark morning. The rays from the sun reached the trees, bursting through the greens, bringing light to the day. Rays of light reflected supremely off the earth; harboring the dawn.

Daylight stretched as the sun continued to rise; finally reaching this broken man's body...curled up along the side of the interstate. The rain beat down on him, beat down on him, and beat down on him. But each faint beat of his heart was weaker than the last.

With the light from the morning sun, the man's limp body caught the eye of a young woman. Her eyes widened as she covered her mouth in shock and raced to the phone to dial 911.

The rain beat down on the earth, beat down on the earth, and beat down on his soul.
Falling.
Falling.
Darkness.

Death and darkness hovering, as the police and paramedics rushed to the scene. The young man dying on the side of the interstate barely drew a faint breath; the drugs flowing through his blood were too lethal for any heart.

"We are all dependent on one another, every soul of us on earth."
-George Bernard Shaw

The first responder parked his cruiser along the embankment as his eyes viewed the heart-stopping scene. Seeing the body, he quickly ran to kneel beside it. Then, as he placed his fingers on the young man's neck to check for vitals, his hand instinctively drew back. There was not even the slightest hint of a pulse, the body felt ice-cold to the touch.

He radioed in the call.

1085 echo.

The code police use for 'dead body.'

The paramedics arrived shortly thereafter, loading the young man's body into the ambulance, providing shelter from the storm. Then the ambulance sped away with its sirens blaring in the otherwise quiet morning.

By this time a small crowd had gathered, displaying looks of fear and despair as the ambulance carted away the lifeless body.

One could only imagine the unspoken pleas of hope that maybe, just maybe, this tragic story could end differently. That this young man could breathe again, and live another day.

The unsung angel who placed the call to 911 looked on with the others, appearing to pray. Then she overheard one of the onlookers say, 'Another one gone. So young, so full of life and opportunity, gone.'

The ambulance rushed onward as the young man lay lifeless on the gurney. The paramedics found no pulse and they knew from their training that there was a slim chance this young man would ever breathe again. If, by some miracle he did, each second that ticked by was further sealing the fate that he'd become a vegetable for the rest of his life.

Inside the ambulance was a young paramedic, on the job his first week. Within him he was filled with fire and energy, fueling a determination to give all he had to this dying young man. That energy, coupled with the strength and wisdom of the other men in the ambulance, created a fearless intensity to do all they could to help save this man's life.

"Never, never, no never give up."
-Winston Churchill

That morning, the heroes in that ambulance never gave up. Moments before arriving at the hospital, the unthinkable happened, his heart began to beat again; life kissed his lips, filling his body, his soul, and his heart.

As the wheels of the ambulance screeched to a stop in front of the doors to the emergency room, the paramedics rushed him inside. Without hesitation, the doctors and nurses became aware of just how delicately this life hung in the balance. Efficiently and naturally they dove into their mission with courage and precision. With each second that ticked by, the precious balance between life and death teetered and tipped.

In his pocket was a folded piece of paper, soaked from the morning rain. The phone number scratched on its surface was barely visible. A member from the hospital staff called the number in hopes of finding a connection.

After a few short rings a young woman picked up. Only a few short moments passed before her heart was crushed by the weight of the news. She had just learned that her big brother was in the emergency room, clawing for life.

He was two years older than her, and through the peaks and valleys of life together, they had become best of friends. They shared a bond unbroken and now in jeopardy of being severed.

She raced to her car, blinded by an indomitable will and determination to be there for her brother. The rain beat down on her windshield as she struggled to see the highway through her tears. She sped into the hospital parking lot and ran through the rain. As she entered the Emergency Room she quickly realized the gravity of the heart stopping scene. Her brother's body was engulfed by violent spasms as the straps across him seemed to barely serve their purpose.

Torment and shock rippled through his body as his mind tip-toed consciousness. Light and dark battled within as he screamed sounds of unintelligible agony and pain.

Amidst the chaos, his brave sister, full of strength and heart, pushed her way through the doctors trying to block her from the room. Tears filled her eyes as the surety of her resolve filled the room. She spoke with clarity, and her word became law. There was no way they were going to make her leave the room.

His body continued to convulse on the gurney. As the doctors and nurses scrambled to do all they could, his little sister reached out to him and held his hand. With all the faith in the world she told him, "Everything is going to be okay." And, in that moment, his convulsing stopped. A comforting peace filled the air and a breath of hope was felt within.

"Faith is the force of life."
-Leo Tolstoy

Somewhere, deep in his subconscious, he could feel the loving hand of his sister pulling for him, praying for him, and hoping for him... with all her heart.

With his convulsing at bay, it gave everyone a moment to absorb the scene. This young man lay there broken. Fear was written across the very fabric of his being. Shock and confusion filled his heart and body. Life or death hung in the balance.

'Was it his time to go?'

The nurses, doctors, and hospital staff worked the miracles of their profession, and did everything within their power. His life was now in '**the hands of a power greater than understanding.**'

As each member of his family was notified a searing pain scarred their hearts. Each one felt the heartache personally, the sting singularly. Everyone asking, "Why did this happen?"

Through the next painstaking hours his family braced themselves for the possibilities. They all learned of the likelihood of him having permanent brain damage, best case scenario. He was gone too long. But still, his family held on, to hope. Hour after excruciating hour.

In a world where it may seem like there is only tragedy and pain around every corner, I am here to tell you there are angels, and heroes, and miracles too. After what seemed like an eternity his heart began to stabilize. The fog and haze in his mind began to clear. Consciousness filled his mind, light and life filled the room, and the darkness of that morning was lit up by the light.

As his vision began to clear he saw that he was surrounded by familiar faces. The experience they were suffering through was written in their eyes. The pain seared on their hearts was visible through the cover of their tears. As they saw recognition and a hint of a smile cross his face, their hearts instantly poured out with gratitude and hope.

He felt the love of his sister, as she held his hand tightly. He noticed her face was drenched in tears. In his mother's eyes, he saw her love and felt her connection to him. He felt her love as he lay there hanging on. He saw the love and hope of his father standing strong and firm, as his heart was breaking on the inside, watching his son, tired and worn, lie still.

With each passing day in the intensive care unit, he was strengthened and blessed. Before long he was permitted a full recovery. It was nothing short of a modern-day miracle. After a few more days, he was cleared to go home.

His blood had pooled to the side of his body that hugged the bank of the interstate that morning, leaving his leg swollen from the fluids that were pumped in him. So, he dragged his left leg across the marble floor, limping, he neared the exit of the hospital. The doors opened and the warmth of the sun washed over his face.

A new beginning, another shot of life.

But the battleground within was still fresh. The wave from his choices still ready to crash down...

Has He Had Enough?

2

'Have I Had Enough?'

"A journey of a thousand miles begins with a single step."
-Lao Tzu

As I related this story every seat in the assembly hall was silent. You could literally hear my heart beating through the microphone; I held onto it so tightly. My emotions felt so close to the surface, so I instinctively paused to catch my breath.

My eyes reflected the eager faces of the young men and women packed into the assembly. I breathed in as my heart raced faster. I could feel the presence of all eyes on me. So, I stood there on stage, alone in the silence. Feeling humbled and broken.

I was flanked to my left by a police escort. It consisted of a wide range of police officers, the lieutenant, and parole officers. Next to them stood some of the school faculty. Everyone waiting patiently as they listened to the story of this young man's overdose.

It must have been an intriguing scene as I stood there on stage in my prison garb. Tailored in a set of Utah Department of Corrections issued prison whites. Property of the state of Utah.

This short trip to the school was my first time out in public in two years. But there I stood, microphone in hand, surrounded by my police escort, and looking directly into the eyes of today's youth.

The weight of the silence in the assembly hall felt almost tangible. I could feel a bead of sweat trickling down my forehead. Then I breathed in another deep breath, I was ready. The experience of my journey led me here, prepared me. I remember looking at the youth in the crowd and wondering what kind of battles they fight.

After a brief pause, my mind's eye focused back to that morning years earlier, lying cold and alone on the bank of the interstate.

Then I felt the strength to go on.

I met the anxious eyes of those in the assembly hall. With as much faith as I could muster, I held their gaze and stated, "The young man from this story is me, I died that day."

The weight of that statement created a flood of memories, flashing vividly in my mind. I could feel the pain leaking out of my eyes.

I regained my composure, then expressed, "Unfortunately for me the battle didn't end there as I walked out of those hospital doors so many years ago. You'd think that close call with death would have been enough. **I guess maybe I just hadn't had enough,** or maybe the pain hadn't stung deep enough yet. Whatever it was, the crippling path of my addiction had only just begun. I was destined to cause another ocean of pain and another mountain of heartache and chaos."

As I verbalized those thoughts it felt good, in a way, to own up to them. The gravity of the situation I'd created, through fifteen years of active addiction, weighed heavily on my mind.

So, there I stood, property of the state, serving a four-and-a-half-year prison sentence. Wondering, 'How did I get so far off? Why do I keep going back? When is enough, enough?

I saw so much hope in the eyes of those students. But, in the subtlest of ways, I could see, hidden behind that hope, a glimmer of the battles they fight. It wasn't so long ago that I was their age, feeling untouchable and invincible, but also so vulnerable within.

I opened the assembly to the audience for questions. As their hands raised we began to carry on a dialogue about some of the choices I made that led me here to prison. Then a young man toward the front raised his hand and asked me a question, with such caring curiosity. He said, "Do you ever still have thoughts to use?"

That question, with all its innocence and simplicity, brought such a profound awakening to my mind regarding the complexity of addiction. I thought, '**Have I had enough..?**' It hit me like a ton of bricks. I'm grateful today for that young man's question, it sparked something within me.

As I answered him I spoke openly about the battle within. About that opposing force in the shadows of my mind, always enticing and seducing. A shape shifting deceptive force constantly trying to lure me off the path. I guess the the key is not listening to those thoughts, not feeding them. Then I talked about the flip-side of that coin, the importance of strengthening who we are and what we stand for. I believe we all have a warrior within us, it just must be realized, then awakened.

As I was transported back to jail I reflected on how out-of-control my life had become. I thought of the direction my life was headed and to where my addiction brought me. The thought came to me again, even more powerfully than before, '**Have I had enough..?**'

In my jail cell that night I stared out of the window, past the chain-link and barb-wire, to the beautiful inviting sky. I felt a deep and comforting peace within me as I reflected on how passionately I wanted to live a good life. I thought of my five-year-old son Dominic and the hurt his heart must be feeling because I'm gone. Then finally, for the first time in my life, I felt a burning desire to LIVE. A comfort came over me, I knew I could awaken my true purpose in life, and change.

That day so many years ago as I lay dying of drug overdose, was not the first time...nor would it be the last.

This is my story...

3

'The Beginning'

"Know Thyself"

(gnothi seaton)

(The words inscribed above the temple of Apollo at Delphi (ancient Greece) sight of the sacred oracle)

As I sit here on my bunk, surrounded by concrete and cinderblock, my mind travels back through the journey that's been my life so far. My mind is flooded with thoughts and memories. I put the pieces together and wonder how much is lost from years of drug abuse.

Sharing my story on these pages has been an interesting endeavor. As you journey with me through the peaks and valleys of my life, some pages will be filled with heartache and pain while my prayer is that others may bring hope and happiness to you.

Writing this has helped me begin to understand who I am, and just how vicious my addiction became. But, like they say, to get where you're headed you've got to know where you've been. I guess it'd be best if we took a brief journey back to the beginning...

I came into this world in March of 1982, the second of four children. I was brought up well, taught the difference between right and wrong. I learned to value family, loyalty, integrity, honor, work, service, and basically everything good.

I sit here today and replay the memories of what feels like another lifetime ago, a time that felt so much simpler. I can still feel the soft leather of my old baseball glove sliding onto my hand as I raced onto the sun-drenched ball field. I remember the smell of the fresh-cut grass and the feeling of dirt under my cleats. Hope and Joy fill my heart as these memories touch my mind.

I can vividly remember the basketball comfortably spinning in my hand, my feet seemed to glide on air as I set up for a jump shot. I played on that old hoop in our concrete driveway; perfecting my shot. Hour after hour, day after day.

I remember the joys and freedoms of summertime. Hiking and fishing with my dad in the mountains. I recall the feeling of the warm summer air, the smell of fireworks, and the taste of moms' homemade ice-cream. The world seemed so inviting back then.

As a family, we did so much together. I remember road-trips during the summer months as we drove cross-country to North Carolina.

I enjoy those family memories. It was always an adventure with mom, she is one of those special spirits who make each moment an adventure.

My parents taught me about service and how to be a survivor. By the time I made it to junior high school, the year was 1995. Thirteen was an awkward age for me, to say the least. I just wasn't sure who I was. I became afraid.

With that fear I began to believe there was something missing, within me. As if I was 'lacking' in some way. I didn't feel comfortable in my own skin. My brain told me that everyone else must have this magical comfort, and I was the only who didn't.

My parents divorced that same year. Leading up to the divorce I remember praying to God to keep my parents together. I prayed with every ounce of my soul. Night after night, day after day. I renounced God when He didn't do what I wanted Him to do. I cut off the conduit. I stopped believing that there was a God who loved me, because He didn't do MY will.

My Dad remarried and it created a joint family with eight siblings in all. My parents and family did well dealing with a difficult situation. Life moved on as we did the best we could. I love my family so much.

I was an active young man. I did okay in school. But during those years I still remember feeling displaced, my spiritual connection was gone, and my brain told me I wasn't enough. I felt something was wrong with my internal makeup.

During my first year of high school I got drunk. I remember finally feeling comfortable in my own skin. I was funny, more relaxed, and I was comfortable. At last, I found what I was missing. I was complete.

I knew what I was doing went against what I was taught, but how could something that feels so good, be so bad... right? So, I compromised. Maybe I was attracted to it. Whatever it was, I was hooked.

That seemingly insignificant compromise with my conscience created a domino effect.

I began seeking more and more. Different drugs with different effects, all to bring me some form of comfort and fill the void I felt.

It was slow at first. I thought I was in control back then, even as I started drinking to oblivion. Almost like it was a game to see how far I could push it. Before long I experienced blackouts, then the haze crept in. My mind was clouded as I slipped further and further into the clutches of my addiction. I was lost.

Take a ride with me.

The car sped down the highway as the shimmer of the Vegas skyline sparkled in my eyes. We weren't even to Las Vegas yet, and there was already an excitement in the air.

Vegas. New Year's Eve. The year 2000. A few hours away from the start of the new millennium.

I was seventeen years old, feeling invincible and untouchable. And I was on a crash course for trouble. The car I rode in sped down the highway as I reached for more pills. I can still recall the sound as the car stereo blared loudly and my crew got pumped for the night. 'Vegas'...one word sums it all up.

My mind was already in a haze by the time we arrived, fueled by a cocktail of drugs. I felt absorbed by the excitement and energy in the air. It's like the energy around me was pumping through me. The cocktail of drugs and alcohol pumped feverishly through my blood.

I remember gazing over the strip as my head nodded off, the lights from the Vegas strip leaving tracers of streaks and streams. Then I was out. No memory, blackout. Later, I experienced a flash of consciousness. I was much further down the strip, surrounded by the lights and smoke, then I was out again.

I woke up the next morning feeling dazed and disoriented. One thing I remember from that morning is laughing about how much of the previous night I didn't remember. With my distorted badge of honor, I bragged to my friends. The sad reality in this story is this was just another day for me, one of so many others lost in a haze. As I tiptoed precariously along the balance of life and death, there was a part of my soul that could feel the impending storm looming ahead. My senior year of high school served as a launch pad for my role as a bonified partier. I quickly became known as the type that would try anything and do anything, if it got me high.

My addiction spiraled out of control so quickly from that point. If there were limits, I pushed them. Every time.

One night I had taken various pills, barbiturates and muscle relaxers, then I mixed them with multiple capfuls of the designer drug GHB. I felt my mind go fuzzy and I knew I was going out. Then, darkness.

I regained consciousness in a room at a hospital, lying on a gurney with nurses leaning over me. I was disoriented but I knew I wanted to get out of there. My body filled with adrenaline as I leapt from the bed and ran for the doors. My legs were running faster than my mind could run, so I stumbled and ran as fast as I could. Finally, disappearing into the darkness.

After running wildly through the night, I discovered that my friends had dropped me off at the doors of the hospital, with the words 'overdose' written on my shirt.

And that was just another night for me. Lost. Tiptoeing the line.

My brain was lying to me. Every time I made a choice that went against what I knew in my heart was right, the next time became easier. My addiction lives in my thoughts and progressively grows stronger when I feed those thoughts, listen to them, believe them, and act upon them. This created a blinding, binding, numbing fog around my mind. I was becoming a man that even I didn't recognize. I numbed my conscience, fueled by pride, ego, and an overall arrogance; creating a blatant disregard for the values I once cherished.

The blackouts continued, the lies got bigger, and the fog in my mind became thick and suffocating. This was my life now. Drugs, and thus, crime.

Overshadowed by the weighty darkness in my mind, the light within my soul didn't reach the surface of my eyes. I could feel the intruding presence of my addiction, but I also felt numb, indifferent, denying any conviction to do something about it.

By May of 2000 I had somehow graduated high school. To this day, I still have no idea how that happened. Nevertheless, following that marvel I had zero plans for my future. College was not on my 'to do list.' My energy gravitated to the criminal underworld.

I started taking frequent trips to Vegas, Southern California, and Mexico. Living a life of drugs and crime I exposed myself to a fearful world. I always felt like I was running from something. It seems the only time I felt any solace was when I inhaled a breath of that captivating California air, finally feeling free for a moment.

The smell of fresh tortillas, salsa, and tequila are fresh in my mind as I recall the memories of walking along the dirty streets of Tijuana. I experienced a new level of danger as darkness engulfed the sunless streets of Mexico. My mind was constantly blinded by a fog of pills and alcohol during my time there. Multiple close calls with the Mexican police, street gangsters, and the U.S. customs agents.

I was addicted to the rush of it all.

Back home in Utah I got arrested, frequently. Late-night parties ended in late-night arrests. Initially the arrests were petty, I was charged with consumption of alcohol by a minor and disorderly conduct. Then to possession of narcotics and interfering with arrest. The criminal charges piled up. Even amidst all this chaos I remember just how in control I felt. Close call after close call. Party after party. Blackout after blackout. The darkness around me got heavier and heavier.

I reached to drugs to numb the pain, creating more pain, reaching to more drugs to numb the deeper pain. The vicious cycle perpetuated.

During that time, I attended a funeral about every month. So many of my friends were dying from drug overdose. The hills of the cemetery filled with their headstones. Overdose after awful overdose, and I just never got the picture. Although the signs were obvious, this could be me, lying there cold in the casket.

By the summer of 2001 I could have wondered, 'Who am I? What do I stand for?' But it's plain to see, I had no clue.

I was about to get a wake-up call.

Have I Had Enough?

4

'The Thunder Rolls'

"Because of the dual constitution of all things, In labor as in life, there can be no cheating; the thief steals from himself, the swindler swindles himself. For the real price of labor is knowledge and virtue, whereof wealth and credit are signs. The signs, like paper money, may be counterfeited or stolen, but that which they represent; namely knowledge and virtue cannot be counterfeited."
-Ralph Waldo Emerson

The warm July air carried the smells of barbecue and firework smoke. For most people, this season is a time for family, freedom, and celebration. But not for me, I was a bound by the chains of my addiction.

The warm summer air rushed past my face as I ran faster than I'd ever run before. My heart was pounding from fear and adrenaline. I ran past street lights and darted through unfamiliar roads. Dressed in black I blended with the night. Clutched firmly in my hands I held a green money bag. The whole police force was in hot pursuit.

I heard people chasing me and the squeal of tires racing towards me. I ducked around corners and hopped over fences.

The valium pumping through my veins clouded my judgement, while the THC slowed my endurance. I found a place to hunker down and prepared to wait it out. My heart beat wildly as I tried to slow my breathing. The sound of police cars speeding around the neighborhood got closer. Then I heard yelling in the distance.

Closer...Closer...
Louder...Louder...

My entire being was seized by fear. I felt paralyzed. My mind began to nod off from the Valium, while my heart continued to pound.

Frozen from fear I crouched as low as I could. I saw the light getting closer and closer. I could hear bushes being ruffled. Then the light from the officer's flashlight grazed me. I froze, and instantly his pistol was pointed at my head. I knew I was done for. I fell to my knees as he cuffed me with speed and precision. I was handcuffed, dragged out to the street, and placed on my knees.

The array of flashlights, headlights, and flashing reds and blues all pointed directly at me, the hooded man. I was blinded by the light and lost in my shame, so I dropped my head in despair.

With my hands cuffed tightly behind my back I finally mustered what little will I had left in me, and lifted my shameful head.

For the crime of robbery, I was sentenced to serve one year in jail. I remember the first day of my sentence. I wasn't sure what to expect so immediately I puffed up with an attitude of pride and arrogance. It could have been a wakeup call for me, but I didn't take it seriously. I guess it's hard to take it seriously if you don't think you have a problem.

After a few months, I was given the opportunity to serve the remaining time in a work-release section. Before long I buckled and started using again. I was sneaking around finding drugs that couldn't be tested on the standard urine test. I even went as far as taking hallucinogenic mushrooms while I was in the jail. I recall laying down on my bunk, feeling paralyzed by fear, as the intensity of the mushrooms sent my mind reeling. I just stared, blankly at the green exit sign, while my mind raced with panic. Ironically, this would be prelude of what was next along my journey.

I reached a point of indifference shortly after that night of magic mushrooms. One of the benefits of being in a work-release section is that you get to leave the jail property for work each day. Instead of heading to work, I decided to head over to a friend's house.

They were all getting high. So, I did what any good addict would do, and I got high too.

Now, I knew I would fail a drug test, and I also knew the officers were vigilant when it came to testing. Therefore, along with that ill-advised choice to get high, I decided not to go back to jail.

They issued warrants and began questioning anyone who knew me. I could feel the pressure and the panic start to kick in. I came to my senses once the drugs wore off a bit.

I felt so trapped and overwhelmed. Facing and accepting responsibility for what I'd done, and continued to do was such a foreign idea to me. I wanted to run and escape it all.

Instead of running I decided to call my mom. After telling her what I was up against she agreed it would be best if I headed back to jail and faced the music. As I rode in the passenger seat I wished that drive could last forever. But, as the car ventured through the cold snowy night, we eventually made it back to jail. I walked up to those doors and before opening them I looked back to my mom. In her eyes, I saw heartbreak mixed beautifully with a glimmer of hope.

I was immediately handcuffed and taken to solitary confinement where I was charged with escape from a correctional facility. As I sat on the cold concrete of that cell I replayed the look I saw in my mother's eyes. There was a part of me, deep down within, that wanted to change. I didn't want to keep disappointing and hurting those that love me. Unfortunately, it was buried under the battlefield that raged in my mind.

My ego stole the show. I puffed up and walked with a chip on my shoulder, wearing a badge of criminal pride. The mask I wore was a façade, I knew that, but my pride was not going to let me admit it. I clutched tightly to the life I was living.

Therefore, my time in jail turned counterproductive. I started making friends with people heading in the wrong direction. My mind would race, late into the night, romancing the time I would be able to get high again. The highs were my treasure. I held onto the memories of them so tightly, relentlessly yearning for the moment my love affair with drugs could be united once more.

During my time in there I remember thinking that if I could just be released then everything would be right in my world. I'll be alright, I've got it all under control.

After a year behind the wall, my time was up. My heart began to pound as I walked down the long corridor to be released. What an exhilarating feeling! Those walls were my cage and I was finally on my way out. As I left the parking lot I felt the warm winds of freedom. My heart rejoiced, I felt alive again! The sights and smells of the city filled my soul with nostalgia. Each of my senses were overloaded with life.

Strolling around the mall for a while gave my senses the ability to relax a bit. I met up with an old friend in the parking lot. And, on my release date from jail, I was introduced to the powerful opioid painkiller, OxyContin. My friends and I would refer to it as 'The Green Monster.' I crushed the Oxy into a fine powder, lined it up on a CD case, then powerfully sniffed the white powder up my nose. Just a few short moments later I was laying on my back, in the grass, puffing on a cigar, feeling like I was floating on the clouds. Literally.

I was higher than I'd ever been, and I loved every second of it. Hooked from the first time it touched my nose. I was on cloud nine. Unfortunately, I'd be chasing the feeling I felt that day for years to come.

My addiction rapidly spun out of control. This time it was quick and it was nasty. It was as if I hadn't missed a beat. Barely out of jail and I was in way over my head. Along with my newfound love affair with painkillers came an insatiable thirst and hunger for more and more. The only time I felt satisfaction was when the powder rocketed up my nose. After that moment of euphoria, my mind would take over. Fear racked my brain, constantly. I would do just about anything to support my addiction, provided the opportunity was there. I continued making trips down south chasing the hunger for more pills. I naturally gravitated toward the life of crime.

By autumn of 2002 I was using well-over a hundred milligrams of OxyContin a day. The brief stints of employment I managed to have never lasted long. I constantly lived in a state of fear and uncertainty. The impending doom I felt continued to compound as I spiraled further into the depths, creating more of what I feared.

Painkillers served as the rudder to my ship, always guiding the direction I was headed. I bounced from job to job, and from house to house. Wherever my addiction took me, I followed. I can only imagine the heartache and pain I caused to those around me. It must have been so devastating to watch me chase the very thing that was killing me. But there was no stopping me now.

In a dense fog of cocaine, ecstasy, pain pills, and alcohol I stumbled across late night parties, more arrests, and new drugs to try. I became a slave to the monster OxyContin.

Meanwhile, a vicious battle was raging in my mind. Thoughts of shame and guilt filled my mind as I thought about the choices I was making, daily.

My addiction told me I wasn't worth it and that change wasn't possible. So, like any good addict, I reached for pain pills to numb the internal pain I felt. But the aid from pain pills was only temporary and created more of the pain I so desperately wanted to escape from.

I was dying inside.

Lies slipped off my tongue with a deceiving swiftness, rotting my moral compass. I scoured the city like a relentless hunter, manipulating and expending any resource I could get. I was in way over my head. These pain pills didn't just change the rules; this was a whole new ballgame.

Then, out of the blue one morning, my fragile little world was rocked to the core. I called a lawyer to seek out representation for some of my previous arrests. He researched my name and came back with some devastating news. Saying, "Ryan, it like looks like you're going to need some serious representation bud, it shows here that you have a warrant out for your arrest. The warrant alleges your involvement in an aggravated robbery. That's a first-degree felony punishable from five years to life in prison."

My heart dropped. Immediately the phone call went silent as I fumbled to hang up. Panic and fear coursed through me. My back slowly inched down the wall as I collapsed to the floor. I knew what this was about, I knew from the second that lawyer uttered those words, but I didn't want to believe it. My choices were finally catching up to me.

This warrant had to do with my involvement in the robbery of a movie theater six-months prior. I remember the crime vividly. With the money, I went straight to my dealer and bought hundreds of OxyContin. Further fueling the ravenous beast of my addiction. And now I'd backed myself into a corner. The walls I created were closing in on me fast. I was lost. I was falling. But I just kept running.

I gathered up my essentials and planned to run south of the border. I felt trapped around every corner I turned. I wanted out of here.

Racked with guilt I began to think of my family and my future. This brought a ray of light into my mind. I remember hearing the song 'Better Off Alone' by Alice DJ and that made me think of my family. These thoughts of family helped me see a ray of light within me. I knew I wouldn't leave the country. So, I stayed.

That February, which was a week before my 21st birthday, I was arrested trying to cash a fraudulent payroll check. I sat, handcuffed in the backseat of a police car feeling the weight of the world on my shoulders. I had so many fake ID's on me that they didn't know who I was. I don't think I even knew who I was. What was I thinking? What have I done? Who had I become? I felt hopelessly lost and spiritually dead. In that moment, I didn't want to live. As I remained cuffed in the back of the squad car, wishing I could somehow open the door and bail in front of a semi as we barreled down the interstate. I wanted to end it.

The darkness, despair, doubt, and fear that coursed through my mind buried my heart and soul. I stared blankly as they booked me into jail and confirmed the warrant I had on me for robbery. After two months in jail I made bail and walked out of those cold steel doors feeling numb and reckless. My eyes glazed over with indifference. My mind had become my own personal hell on earth. All the choices I made over the past few years filled me with regret.

I compromised with my conscience and it turned me farther from the light. Those deceptive thoughts of doubt and despair crept into my mind, and I listened to them. I believed them. The battle I fought within was taking over. I reached a point where I didn't care whether I lived or died.

I believe that opposing force in my mind saw the prime time to strike, because just a few short days later I would be lying on the embankment of the interstate, dead.

Have I Had Enough?

5

'1085 Echo'

"Addiction is dealing with that hole in the soul."
                                        -William Moyers

The air of indifference followed me as I walked from the jail on to my mission. My heart was cold to the world. During the next passing day, I numbed myself with drugs and alcohol, which iced over my heart and my will to press forward.

I created isolation from family and all those who love me. I guess I was too prideful to reach out. In my mind, all hope was lost

As if it were a pre-destined ritual, I got in the car and headed to the city. Picking up over one-hundred balloons of cocaine. I don't remember feeling any trepidation or regret, not even any worry. My back was to the world and I just didn't give a f****.

My soul was numb because my mind was cold.

That night I sat at a table holding a bottle of *Ice 101*, bottoms up. The frost from the bottle chilled my hand, as the thick cold liquor washed down the back of my throat it carried with it another handful of pills.

I sat there at the table carelessly indifferent to the party surrounding me. They danced and they laughed as the music played in the background. My eyes, bloodshot and glazed over, took my thoughts a million miles away. I sniffed line after line of cocaine. I was relentless, a man on a mission. I chased each line of cocaine with a line of Oxy, which masked the burn as the cocaine dripped continuously down my throat. Subconsciously I knew what I was doing, although consciously I was masking it with feelings of invincibility.

I swallowed more pills. A few Xanax, a couple more Valium. Each time I chugged more liquor it would wash the raw drip from the back of my throat. Line after line of cocaine quenched the hunger I felt, and then so quickly, I felt the hunger and need again. So, I chopped up more lines to quench the thirst.

From this point, I began to fade in and out of consciousness. I have a fleeting glimpse of me being in a car swallowing a few Dilaudids, then I was out again.

I was defeated before I began that day. The drugs were merely the means.

Somehow, I made it back to the party, immediately finding the nearest liquor bottle and washing the burning liquid down my throat. I remember looking around at the others at the party, all the dancing and laughing seemed so counterfeit to me. Like they were all puppets on a string. And there I sat, the biggest puppet of them all.

I felt sick as I stood up. My stomach seized and moaned, but I began walking, immediately I felt dizzy as my head rushed with toxic blood. All I saw was darkness as I attempted to clear my vision. I slowly inched my way down the hall bouncing from wall-to-wall like a pinball in slow-motion. Gradually I made my way out.

With the bottle of alcohol clutched firmly in my grasp I opened the door to leave the party. The fresh air was inviting as it hit my face, a welcome change from the smoke-filled rooms. I sauntered down the walkway, an aimless fool hopelessly lost. I felt my resolve strengthen as I tipped the bottom of that bottle up, one last time. Then, I took off running. I don't know what the force was that drove me. Was it fear? Was it adrenaline mixed with the thick cocktail of drugs coursing through my blood? Or, maybe it was a need to escape, to run, and to fade away into the blackness.

Whatever it was, I ran, stumbled, and I ran some more. Then I came to a fence that separated the city from the interstate. I jumped to it and began to climb, but my mind went dark as I tried to vault from the top. I tripped on my way over the fence, and I fell hard, my face slamming into the mud along the bank of the interstate.

I was out cold.

My mind had lost all consciousness as the rain pattered across my face and my heart struggled to continue beating. I struggle with the words to portray exactly what my soul experienced as I lay there nearing my death. But I know I felt dark, a dense mist of pain gnashing at my soul. It's as if I could feel the claws of death literally scraping for my life. Those feelings I experienced somewhere so deep in my awareness that morning, continue to scare me to this day.

But after the dark of that night I began to feel a resounding peace around me. I felt an eternal love. I could feel the love of my family. The prayers from so many gave me strength. While I was strapped to the hospital bed and battling with consciousness, my sister was holding my hand, unbeknownst to me at the time. Somewhere deep in my subconscious I could feel her faith, her love, and her hope.

I began to stabilize. My mind filled with the spirit of consciousness. I looked around the hospital room and saw so many familiar faces. Recognition had just entered my mind and life was in my eyes. Through the lens of tears, I could see joy and love in their eyes.

We cried tears of joy together, tears of hope, tears of heart-ache, tears of pain. And we cried because of love. That day was full of so many miracles. My life was touched by angels and heroes, and blessed so intimately by prayer. I believe my **God** blessed me with another chance.

I felt a newfound strength as I was released from the hospital. Walking toward the exit I felt humbled and renewed. I dragged my left foot across the marble floor and limped my way toward the beautiful morning sunshine.

I felt a glimpse of light. I felt hope. I felt love.

My Dad and I drove out of the hospital parking lot heading directly to the fire station. We planned to speak with the paramedics who so valiantly gave their all to help save my life. As we entered the station there was an interesting silence. Maybe they could see the IV marks on my body from the hospital. At first, they just looked confused but slowly the confusion turned to shock as they made the connection in their minds. Realizing that I was the young man they scooped up from the side of the interstate a week ago, with no pulse and no chance. I extended my hand to theirs and thanked them with tears of gratitude filling my heart. One of the paramedics just stood there in awe, then finally saying, "No way man, I can't believe it's you. As we dropped you off at the hospital we knew, if by some miracle, you lived, you'd be a vegetable for the rest of your life."

I left there feeling deeply humbled that I'd been blessed with another shot at life. Something changed within me that day. I could've died that day. The science of it says, I should have died that day.

Have I Had Enough?

6

'Like a Dog to his Vomit'

"As a dog returneth to his vomit, so a fool returneth to his Folly."
-Proverbs 26:11

    I recovered from the overdose rather quickly, at least physically. Before long I had all the movement back in my leg and felt physically adept. But my emotional and spiritual recovery was a different story. I felt scattered, uncertain, confused, and conflicted. My brain filled with doubts and worries. I felt like I wanted to change my ways, but all the legal and criminal consequences created a whirlwind of stress. With my willpower alone I wouldn't get very far.

    Although I wanted to change, I still had thoughts and habits engrained within me through years of addiction. I chose to feed those thoughts. Out of habit, those thoughts became my master.

After a few court appearances and feeling the weight of responsibility baring down on me, I began to think about ways I could escape. I wanted to run, again. Or at least find a way to pay off the court system and be done with it. Looking back, I see how much I blamed the court system for my trials.

"Habit is either the best of servants or the worst of masters."
-Nathaniel Emmons

I remember reading through my court papers, staring blankly at all the debt I was in, and listening to the constant hum of negativity that reverberated in my brain. My addiction lives in my thoughts, and it was relentless. A constant obsession of the mind, 'You're not worth it Ryan, you're in too deep, numb your pain, nobody understands you, there is no other way, you deserve to feel good, try it, just for tonight.' On and on, the thoughts pounded my brain.

I started sneaking around and lying to those closest to me. I lied to, manipulated, and deceived all those around me. I was so quick to forget. The choices I abegan to make created more guilt and pressure, adding to the dense cloud of fear within me. In my mind, I knew I had to escape. So, I reached for what I knew would numb the pain. Returning, 'like a dog to his vomit.'

I was dead on the side of that cold and lonely interstate only a few short months ago, and here I was again, face-to-face with a line of OxyContin. I felt guilty even before I sniffed the Oxy, but the decision was already made, I was committed, there's no turning back now. I felt a moment of escape as the white powder blasted up my nose and down the back of my throat. Only a few short minutes later I began to understand just how in over my head I was.

The guilt I was creating brought even more shame, causing me to reach even further to numb the pain. I was in a full-blown relapse. Those enticing whispers of the opposing force were relentless, and they didn't let up. My addiction whispered, 'you need to get high to function, people only like you when you're high, you can get away with it, you're fooling everyone, it's who you are." Each whisper led me further away from the light.

From that point, I basically threw in the towel. With the looming court case hanging over my head I reverted to my old ways, creating my own little hell on earth, again. The lies got bigger as my drug abuse progressed. Within me I harbored a deepening interior list of all my failures, lies, and shame. I held on to those secret burdens so tightly. They were killing me from the inside.

I was feeding the opposing force instead of feeding the light. The battle within became grossly overmatched, and I spiraled viciously out of control. I didn't even know what side I was on anymore.

It didn't take long for my fragile little world to come crashing down, again.

Around four o'clock a.m. on a snowy November morning in 2003, I was passed out on a hotel bed in the secluded resort town of Park City, Utah. The drugs and alcohol that coursed through my blood helped ease me to sleep hours before. The scene around me was dismal, bleak at best. Empty corona bottles were placed carelessly on the tables and stools. Clothes were scattered from the bed to the floor and amidst the half empty beer bottles on the coffee table, there were a few stacks of counterfeit twenty dollar bills. The laptop on the table was still playing music and the screen held scanned images of the bills.

My body lie there, eyes heavy, as my mind danced through dreamland. The first thing I heard was the jarring explosion of the flash-bang grenade. Then I heard what sounded like a whole platoon moving through the hotel with swift precision. "Clear! Clear!" My mind snapped awake as my body was being flipped over, handcuffed, and surrounded by the swat team and two Secret Service agents. This all happened simultaneously, within seconds.

I looked up at the badges and guns around me, immediately dropping my head in defeat. An intense wave of nausea rippled through my stomach as a feeling of complete and utter despair filled every ounce of me.

I was interrogated until the sun came up but the fog and haze in my mind had me staring blankly at the interrogating officer. When the morning rays lit up the snowy Park City streets, I stepped into the police car and headed to jail.

I walked into the holding cell and slouched into a stoop. The cold concrete seemed inviting compared to the cold confines of my heart. Bits and pieces of the past six months flashed in my mind; my drug overdose, my relapse on pain pills, and my decision to link up with a few friends and start counterfeiting currency. It all seemed so transparent now, when at the time, I felt so justified by what I was doing. My addiction had deceived me once again.

My thoughts, habits, friends, choices, and values all centered around this lifestyle of getting high and figuring out a way to feed the high. The negative cycle perpetuated a vicious tailspin. I thought I knew who I was but even I didn't recognize the man I'd become.

Now, not only was I facing the movie theater robbery charge, but I was facing the consequences of this new mess.

The insidiousness of my addiction is I create more of the same problems I run from. One of the reasons I decided to get into the counterfeiting business was my brain told me it was a great idea, a way I could finally buy my way out of the trouble I was already in.

A solid dose of reality smacked me upside the head as I watched the story unfold on the ten o'clock news that night from jail. There I was on the TV screen. Busted.

I was bound in every way. Internally I felt the chains bound tightly on my heart, while I felt the cold steel of shackles and chains as they gripped tightly on my ankles and wrists. I was facing multiple felony charges in two separate counties.

Shackled in the transport van I rode along those canyon streets and wondered, 'What happened to the man I used to be? What happened to the boy on the ball field with all the hope of the world?

Have I Had Enough?

7

'Blinded'

"If you don't set a baseline standard for what you'll accept in your life, you'll find it easy to slip into behaviors and attitudes or a quality of life that is far below what you deserve."

-Anthony Robbins

As the months of incarceration slowly ticked by, I began awakening from some of the fog that clouded my mind, helping me to see things more clearly. Although I was in jail, I felt good again. I believe that was because I was inching my way toward the realization that I had a problem. My mom came up to visit often and we talked of goals, of purpose, of passion, and of the warrior within. I cherish those talks with my mom.

During that time, I started making some commitments, one of those was that I'd give up the life of crime. And, unbeknownst to me, the validity of that commitment would forever change the course of the rest of my life.

Looking back on that time time I spent in jail, I can see just how sly and convincing my addiction was. You see, even though I committed to leaving behind the life of crime, I still entertained thoughts of drinking alcohol and using drugs again. I romanced the times when I could use again. My addiction whispered, 'This time will be different, because if I'm not committing any crime I won't get into any trouble, you can still drink, get high, you need it.' Those enticing whispers continued to caress me with their trance, and after a year of jail, I was released. During that year, the charge I faced for robbing the movie theater was dismissed for lack of evidence. I felt relieved, but I also felt the seeds of guilt begin to grow inside me. I knew I'd gotten away with one.

So, I walked out of those doors a free man, with the foreboding words from the Secret Service agent echoing in my mind, 'If I ever see another counterfeit bill with your signature on it, I'm coming for you... full force buddy!" Those words, and my commitment to leave behind the life of crime, helped me to get serious.

I moved in with my sister and her fiancé, got a job, and I worked on my goals. I began to feel a sense of accomplishment. It was a happy time for me in my life. I even started feeling in complete control again. The pain from my past seemed like a fleeting memory. At times, I even felt like the pain was just a long-lost dream, hidden in the dark recesses of my mind.

Before long, I started drinking on the weekends. After all, I deserved to drink, right? When I drank, I drank hard. To the point of blackout often. The lies I told myself continued to grow. My addiction whispered, 'since I'm away from the life of crime I'll be able to maintain, I'm not hurting anyone but myself.' The lies I told myself became deep and bold.

Binge drinking on the weekends turned to binge drinking on the weekdays. With that much drinking I was bound to get hungover, and with the hangover came the pain pills. I used them and within days I was right back into the madness. I would stumble into my sales job and get even more loaded. It was all under the self-imposed illusion that I was *maintaining* or *functioning*. As the months progressed I started dropping ecstasy on the weekends. Then I started using cocaine regularly. I always topped off the night with a cozy concoction of alcohol and pain pills.

About a year of partying went by without any criminal trouble. I finally had it all figured out. During that year, I used almost every single day. I fed myself the story that, since I was working and not committing crime, everything would be just fine. Believing I was in complete control of my addiction.

Under my drug use I buried the guilt I felt. I was so quick to forget.

Things looked great from the outside. Work was going well, I was experiencing a level of success, and I was staying out of trouble. But, *within,* the scene was much different.

My mind felt the churn of guilt and fear, slowly stirring the steaming pot of turmoil inside me. I remember feelings of invincibility, displaying a blatant disregard for the natural rules of life. Those blinding shadows of invincibility signified a time of vulnerability within me.

My ego was in the driver's seat while my soul was merely a passenger, at the mercy of *me*.

During this time, the ever-present beast in the shadows lie lurking, raging, and whispering. An opposing force, methodically calculating the next move and the prime time to strike.

So, I blazed the path ahead, running on my will, inching along, going to work, using and abusing drugs, and floating through my existence. I was getting annihilated on the battlefield within. The cunning element behind it all was that I was too numb to care.

Then, I met a special woman named Bianca. We did everything together. When I was with her I felt like I was on top of the world. We started dating and I felt like I had it all figured out. After all, on the outside everything looked great. I was dating a beautiful young lady, work was going well, and I was staying out of trouble. But on the inside, I still felt hollow, like I was cheating life. I was going against what I knew in my heart to be right. I'd compromised with my conscience, but I was still experiencing a form of success and happiness. Because of that, I knew deep this happiness would only be temporary.

I was a fraud, within. The depth of my character was rotting, and out of shame I hid the reality of the fierce battle I was fighting. I hid it from everyone. At times, I would experience a brief wake up call, but I was quick to reach for drugs to drown the promptings from my soul. The tally of friends we buried was always increasing. I attended funeral after funeral. One drug overdose after the other.

I remember standing over the casket of a good friend of mine, feeling numb from the Hennessy and pills in my blood, wanting to stop, but knowing I was lost.

Each of those caskets could have been holding me. The way I was living it would only be a matter of time, and I couldn't find it in me to heed the promptings I felt. When I thought of the overdoses of my past I felt like they happened to a distant person in another lifetime, almost as if they didn't exist. I blocked it all out of my mind. The guilt I felt each time I sniffed a line was so intense that instinctually I numbed it with more and more. Again, numbing the pain I created with the same thing that caused the pain. My addiction grew and grew, worse than ever before.

The seasons changed and another year passed by with my mind in a fog. Bianca and I continued to share the highs and lows of our journey together. Our relationship strengthened and I began to be more open. Though I still held on to so many secrets. Those secrets spawned even more guilt, thus perpetuating the cycle.

I continued to shun away the many awakening promptings I felt from my soul. My thoughts and energy were consumed by my ego. I was lost in the sea of my addiction, and headed for deeper water. By the time I made it to bed each night I had ingested so many drugs. I used painkillers, day-in and day-out, hour after hour. I knew something had to change, but I was trapped in the clutches of my addiction.

As autumn approached, the winds of the 2006 summer began to cool. Another season of change. And, for me, those winds of change came with yet another call to *awaken*.

Like a long-lost friend, my past finally came back for me.

While I was at work I saw two uniformed police officers talking to the secretary, fear came over me as she pointed directly toward me. I felt their gaze and instinctually knew they were here for me. My first thought was to run, then I just felt confused, after all, what could this be about?

The decision to go speak with them didn't come easy, but I nervously walked toward the officers. My stomach sank as they told me they were here to subpoena me for an upcoming court date. The State of Utah had refiled the robbery charge from the movie theater years ago. My heart sank but there was a part of me that knew it would eventually come back to haunt me. I knew I'd gotten away with one, and here it was again, staring right back at me.

I stood there, alone in the parking lot, filled with fear and uncertainty, watching the sunset. In the silence, my mind raced a thousand miles an hour while I inhaled cigarette after cigarette.

I was, once again, facing five years to life in prison...

Have I Had Enough?

8

'I am in Complete Control'

"For all the words of tongue or pen, the saddest are these:

It might have been."
                                        -John Greenleaf Whittier

The only thing on my mind as I left that parking lot was how fast I could get high. I lashed out, and it was quick and nasty. I started using hundreds of milligrams of Oxy each day. Usually chased with cocaine and alcohol. I used from sun up to lights out.

My eyes reflected the death I felt on the inside as I did some of the most hurtful things to the ones I claimed to love, pushing everyone away. I was a one man wrecking ball, leaving behind an ocean of tears and a wake of heartache.

I began mixing cocaine with heroin. I thirst for it each day. I was heartless and felt hopeless. A loser, barely hanging by a thread, way past the point of desperately needing help.

I lost the woman who loved me, I broke her heart. One night I remember feeling so hollow, empty, cold, and alone as my mind filled with noise and chaos. So, to quiet the noise in my mind I finally knelt and prayed from my heart. I don't remember what was said but I remember what I felt.

A seed of faith was planted inside me that night. I began to see that I couldn't do it alone. And I finally began to glimpse the fact that I seriously needed help. It was time to try something different. I felt the warrior within me begin to stir somewhere deep down.

That night I spoke with Bianca about the pain I caused her and we discussed each other's hopes and dreams. We even talked about the pending court case I had looming in the future. And after all the pain I put her through, even with all the tears, and all heart-ache; she looked me straight in the eyes and said, "I'll stand by you."

I didn't deserve that forgiveness and love but she freely gave it anyway. Still to this day I'm learning just how much of a gift good people are on this earth. If only every man could come across a woman like her, even just once-in-a-lifetime.

With that miracle, my fragile world was coming back together. I felt a glimmer of hope begin to shine from within, and although I wanted a better life, my addiction continued to whisper and I couldn't let go of the drug life. I wouldn't *fully* let go.

And so, those infamous dark clouds of my addiction stirred in the distance. To compromise I substituted my addiction to painkillers with the drug Suboxone. The whispers of my addiction told me, *'I'm in control, I'm not hurting anyone, I need it, this is who I am, it helps me be the man people love.'*

These lies pressed my mind fervently, making me feel like I was suffocating. The whispers of the opposing force were tireless in their approach. I listened to those thoughts and even believed them. To numb the pain, I started binge drinking. The steaming pot of turmoil calmed temporarily, but by the morning I felt the pain even more. I was dead to any purpose in life. I was asleep and numb, drifting through the haze of my existence.

As fate would have it, I was blessed again with another call to action. It came in the news that we were expecting a baby. A wide range of the deepest emotions came over me when I heard the news. I knew this was the time in my life where I was supposed to grow so I could teach him, provide for him, be present in his life, and love him unconditionally. This was supposed to be my time to step up and raise my son.

Things began to look great again, on the outside. Work was going well, I was with a beautiful young lady, we were expecting a child, creating memories, and beginning our little family. But on the inside I was holding on to so many lies. The guilt weighed heavy on my heart. I was dying inside and trying to hold it together.

This was also an exciting time in my life. As I awaited the birth of my son I was filled with a special anticipation and hope. I fondly remember a trip Bianca and I took to the solitude of Southern California.

The ride down there was full of laughter and excitement. We walked the glamorous streets of Rodeo Drive and ate in classic Beverley Hills. I promised her the world as we walked the sun-soaked sands. Just two people in love, soaking up the magnificent California sun. The weather was enchanting and the energy in the air captivated my heart. I was on top of the world. I was about to be a father and I was walking down the sunny pier with an amazing woman. Maybe everything in my world was finally going to be ok...

We watched the sun paint beauty across the sky as it set so majestically in the west. That moment was surreal and I wished I could stop the hands of time. As the sun was setting we made our way to the end of the pier and headed inside a restaurant, I sat down and ordered a Corona with lime. I distinctly remember feeling the cold Corona wash down the back of my throat as my addiction whispered, *'This is perfect, I'm in control, I've got this, I'm going to be just fine.'*

As we returned from our getaway I quickly began to feel the financial pressures looming overhead and the fear from my pending court case was a constant weight.

The commitment I made to leave behind the life of crime was put to the ultimate test. It came on a day when I least expected it. I heard the doorbell ring and when I answered it I saw an old friend of mine standing at the doorway. He looked disheveled and scattered. I hesitated even answering the door. I'd been ignoring his call for what seemed like months.

Finally, I decided to step out on the porch and see what was going on. First, he guilted me for never answering my phone then we made some small talk until he got down to his actual purpose for showing up at my home.

He and another old friend of mine had been up to no-good. As of late they'd been involved in a string of bank robberies and he expressed his desperate need for help on the next one, then he persuasively offered me the job. I must admit, the promises of fast money appealed to me. I could feel the old me trying to surface once again as the enticing whispers of my addiction urged me to say yes.

My mind was filled with those seductive whispers, *'Just this last time, you'll get away with it, think of how many problems that money would solve, you can buy your way out of the other trouble you're in, you'll get away with it, say yes! One and done.'*

Oh! Those enticing thoughts we're so persuasive!

I had a decision to make, then and there. Would I stay true to my commitment or would I buckle and go back to my old ways? Would I choose, in that moment, to risk it all? I thought of the life I had waiting for me inside the house. I thought of my unborn son and I began to feel the warrior within me begin to stir from his slumber.

I had two forces tugging in my mind. It was time to decide.

Have I Had Enough?

9

'The Light of Life'

"Never give up what you want most, for what you want in the moment."

-unknown

I was at a crossroads in my life. I knew, all too well, the darkness leading down one path, and I saw glimpses of light up ahead on the other. I stood there in silence on the porch for a while, feeling the pressures of the opposing force hammering my thoughts as my old friend pressured me to go back to my old ways. In that crucial minute, I was blessed with a moment of strength. I believe it was God that strengthened me. It's as if I saw clearly where each path led. Finally, I replied with all the faith I could muster, "I'm heading in a different direction now man. I have a family. No, count me out."

As I look back on that conversation now it seems like the choice should have been so easy to make. But I remember, in that moment, saying no was one of the hardest things for me to do.

I can't explain why it was so hard for me to stand up for what I knew in my heart was right, but it was. I began feeling stronger immediately after my old friend walked away.

I inched my way back inside the house and fell into Bianca's arms. I remember feeling an intense flush of emotion as I felt her love and concern for me. With worry she asked me what was wrong, and in response I just held her heart next to mine for a while longer, then said, "I love you B."

Not long after, we watched their arrests and convictions play out on the local news. In the end, that old friend of mine was sentenced to forty-six years in federal prison. If I would have said yes, I would have been right there with him. My unborn son would have grown up fatherless. My life and the lives of all those who care for me would have been changed forever. Today I am so grateful for that moment of strength.

That small victory encouraged me, but the battle I face within continued with relentless approach.

My son was heading to this world in just a few short months and I was still abusing painkillers daily. I repeatedly told myself that I would stop, cold turkey, the day my son was born. I decided to use that hollow commitment as a justifiable reason for me to party every day like it was my last. One last hurrah. I held on to the reasoning that, since I was going to quit, I may as well enjoy this last bender.

I partied hard during that time and my work suffered. I used the sales office as my personal place of refuge to get loaded and wasted. I was already behind financially and with the pending court case I was digging my family even further into a hole.

Relationships with my family were stressed in ways that only those close to an addict can understand. It must have been so tough for them to watch someone they love; change into someone they didn't even recognize.

I'd lost my grip on reality, slipping, falling, and lost in the haze. There were times I would tell myself that I would change as soon as my son was born, and a part of me deep down wanted to believe that, but only time would tell. And one late August evening that day came, my unborn son was ready to enter the earth.

A nervous excitement came over me as we entered the hospital, got our room, and prepared for this special time. As we settled into our room late that night I knew a beautiful time was upon us. We prayed together in the early morning hours before our eyelids got too heavy. That prayer brought peace to my heart. Finally, the weight on my eyelids brought a few moments of rest.

On that August morning in 2007 our beautiful prince came into this world. Bianca was so strong, valiant, and beautiful that day. We were all supported by our families with grace. We named him Dominic. I felt so proud as a new father. Feelings I've never felt before rushed through me as I held this precious boy in my arms. His life and his well-being are in my hands.

I felt a love that only a parent can feel, as his heart beat next to mine. I felt his fragile breath exhale across my cheek as his his little hands and fingers stretched for the first time. I looked deep into his beautiful eyes and saw recognition and hope. I felt a calling like I'd never felt before and a love like I'd never known as his precious spirit lit up the room. A protective calling to be a warrior in his life, a hero to him, to provide for him, and to be a man he can always count on.

That was the best day of my life. I was showered with love that day and felt so proud to be this little man's father. But somewhere deep within me I also felt scared and vulnerable.

By nightfall, the sun had long since disappeared, and I sat alone in the bathroom and cried. I walked out of the hospital doors, unsure of what exactly was driving me or what I felt, parked my car and pulled out a CD case. Held in my hands was eighty milligrams of OxyContin. I gently removed the time release coating off the potent painkiller as my addiction whispered, *'I'm in control, I need this, I'll stop as soon as I'm out of this bottle of pills.'* In a trance as my thoughts guided me I crushed the pill into a fine powder. There was no stopping me. I was led by an unquenchable thirst. I sniffed the powder and felt the thick and comforting dust coat the back of my throat.

It pains me to write that even on the best day of my life, when the sun shined so bright, the dark clouds of my addiction still cast a dark shadow within me.

I drove back to the hospital wearing a mask that hid all my lies. I smiled and walked in the doors...

Have I Had Enough?

10

'Dark Clouds'

'If not now, when?'
-Zen Meditation (Hillel the Elder)

When it comes to making changes, tomorrow never comes. Tomorrow turns into next week, next week turns into next month, and before you know it, another year has passed. I chose to cloud the brightest day of my life. Then I chose to keep going.

Tomorrow never came...

When that bottle of pills was gone, I found more. I was driven by an insatiable thirst and hunger. I tried desperately to fill the bottomless void, only to come up short, every time. As the high from the pills wore off I was left unsatisfied and always wanting more. Each time I got high I made an empty promise that it would be my last, but I just kept falling, deeper into my addiction.

I listened to those whispers from the opposing force, *'Quit tomorrow, you deserve to get high today, you need it to function, you need it to provide, everything is going to be ok, just one more.'* On and on, minute after minute, those thoughts caressed me, deeper.

My court dates came and I continued to contest the charges against me. I appeared at court hearings weekly. The possibility of prison time was always looming in the back of my mind. I always tried to block out that reality with my incessant drug abuse.

I was living a double life.

At home I was the loving father and husband. I loved watching my son experience this new world for the first time. I was enthralled by his captivating personality. I cherished the moments I held him close to me and rocked him to sleep in the middle of the night. I loved watching the expression in his eyes as he discovered his surroundings. He is one of those special souls who can light up any room. He's my baby boy.

But, I was a different person when I left to work. I was driven by my drug use. I was *always* high. If not, I was *desperately* searching.

My drug abuse progressed rapidly. I was losing a grip on everything. During this time, I started smoking crack cocaine. And I was addicted to all kinds of pills. I used *Xanex* to help me sleep, *Valium* to calm my nerves, *Adderol* to wake me up, pain pills to even function, ecstasy to make me feel good, and I drank liquor like a fish.

It was a very dark time for me.

While I was in the process of losing my job, I managed to lose our home, and get our car repossessed. I blamed all these problems on the economy and any other reason, if the blame wasn't on me. My little family was experiencing the pain of uncertainty and all I could do was lie to cover up more lies. I was completely out of control and I was breaking hearts all around me as I recklessly walked the line of life and death. It was only a matter of time before I fell.

And that day came.

One night, at work I'd been eating muscle relaxers and drinking *GHB*. After work I went out to eat with some family and snuck out to my car to drink more *GHB* in the parking lot. My mind became cloudy as I took more pills. I remember nodding off in the back of the car before I was dropped off at a baby shower. Bianca was there with our son and she was ready to go home. By my slurred speech, she could tell I was on something. I was acting strange.

I sat in the passenger seat on the ride home. I vaguely remember nodding in and out. I recall Bianca's persistent pleas, 'What's wrong Ryan? What's wrong!? What did you take!?' But as we drove further my mind continued to lose focus. I couldn't snap out of it. I drooled and mumbled incoherently, 'I'm okay, I'm okay, just tired.' After that slur I nodded out again. I was a hot mess. Next thing I remember was sitting in the car, we had stopped somewhere and I was trying to find my bearings. I knew I was someplace familiar, but I couldn't make out where. In the distant recesses of my mind I could hear Bianca's heartfelt cries of worry and heartache. Then, I nodded out again.

I woke up to a bright light shining powerfully into my eyes, a badge, and a policeman holding my eyelids open.

He shined his flashlight in my eyes but I was so far gone that I couldn't form any words. Then I saw the paramedics. I heard questions but I couldn't find the answers, my mind was so confused and disoriented. The only thing I could say was, 'I'm okay...tired.

The questions flew at me, "What's your birthday? How many fingers am I holding up? What did you take?" My mind drew blanks. I couldn't compose a single thought. Nothing.

My mind was spinning. I felt so sick. I couldn't move any part of my body. I was incapacitated. Then I was out again. I remember seeing the roof of the ambulance and the faces of the paramedics peering down as they worked to stabilize me.

I felt panic and confusion deep down within. I was disoriented. I didn't know where I was or what had happened. It's like my mind knew but it couldn't compose a single thought. Panic seized me and then I went out again.

I remember brief flashes of the ambulance ride, then I was in the emergency room with IVs in me. I was surrounded by doctors and nurses that were administrating shots, tests, and stabilizers. I felt a thick black charcoal drink going down my throat and all I could do was slur the words, "I'm okay, just tired." Then, out of nowhere, I felt the strangest pain below my waist. I screamed, "Oooowwwwhhhh!!" The nurse had just put a catheter in me. And that, my friend, helped snap me into reality! I pled desperately with them, 'I'm okay, I'm okay, take it out!'

I quickly began to discover the situation I was in. It all hit me like a ton of bricks. I hung my head and thought, 'What have I done?'

Mom, Bianca, and my little sister came into the room. I could see worry, fear, shock, and confusion racking their hearts and souls. I was single-handedly putting them through a literal hell on earth.

I recovered quickly. The doctors couldn't figure out what had happened, they called me their mystery man.' But I had a little secret, the drugs I was on didn't show up on the standard test. I lied to everyone and told them all I didn't know what happened. I even went as far as suggesting that it could have been an effect from the seizures I used to have as a kid.

Upon my release from the hospital that night and I continued to churn the pot of lies. I felt completely drained and sick. The root of the sickness I felt was that I knew how much of a fraud I was. I was once again breaking hearts all around me. Those who loved me and cared for me were never safe from the worry and fear that, one day soon, I'd be gone forever. I was slowly killing myself.

As we drove away I couldn't help but notice the hospital disappearing in the rearview mirror. When only a few short months ago, those rooms had helped give life to my precious son. And now, those same rooms, just helped save my life.

Have I Had Enough?

11

'The Sound of Total Devastation'

"Addiction is an adaptation.

It's not you—it's the cage you live in."

-Johann Hari

What was I thinking? Hadn't I just become a father? How close did I have to get to death, to decide I wanted to live? *When is enough, enough?*

I was a disheveled mess, digging my family into a hole, all while a constant tangle of lies spewed from my lips. Our other car was repossessed a few days after I was released from the hospital.

I picked up a rental car and headed up to work in a desperate need to make some money. I was barely hanging on while my mind oozed with desperation.

The opposing force was relentless with the whispers, *'You need the pills, you need to drink, it's the only way you can function, block the pain, numb your feelings, it doesn't matter, once you get high everything will be better.'*

A few days later I picked up the same combination of drugs that landed me in the hospital just a few days before. And the whispers continued, *'you know your limits, you'll be okay this time, you need it.'*

That night at work I got loaded on muscle relaxers, *Suboxone,* and *GHB.* After work I sat behind the wheel in the parking lot and continued to get even more wasted. As the music played I could feel the heightened intensity of the *GHB* coursing through my blood, and for a moment I felt good again.

Then I decided to put the car in gear and take off. In a blur, the streams from the city lights flew by me. Thankfully, my mind grew frustrated by the persistence of the infamous seatbelt beep. I grudgingly fastened my seatbelt as I entered the freeway. I was cruising by the time I hit the fast lane. I had my music up, full-blast, and had the pedal to the metal as I whizzed past the other traffic. I was driving recklessly and feeling untouchable. I decided to make a quick stop off one of the exits to meet up with a friend. I drank another cap of G and popped a few more pills. The last cap of G hit me fast and hit me hard, so I left quick and avoided the freeway.

My mind became increasingly cloudy as I stuck to the back roads. My head started nodding out and I got disoriented quick. The back roads all started looking the same, nevertheless, I raced onward.

Fueled by some kind inherent will to just keep going. As I drove faster I began to feel an undercurrent of panic and fear. I was lost, had no clue where I was, and the world around me was spinning increasingly faster by the second. I saw flashes of stop signs and streetlights as I continued to drive. The car barreled faster and faster through the night streets as my foot pressed harder on the accelerator.

The world kept spinning faster and faster. Then, all I heard was silence, all I felt was blackness.

Darkness and silence.

Silence and darkness...

Somewhere far away, in a dark corner of my consciousness, I could feel the speed of the car flying out of control at sixty miles per hour. But all I saw was the blackness, all I felt was the silence.

Then, like the sound of a loud noise awakening you from a dream, I felt the impact and heard that piercing sound of total devastation. My mind was jarred and I began to see stars. I smelled smoke and chemicals. I was surrounded by dust and darkness. Disoriented and lost, I tried to turn the ignition, nothing. I tried again, nothing. Then, I heard voices in the darkness, asking if I was okay. People were running toward me out of the darkness. The only thought I had was that I needed to get out of there, fast. I tried the ignition again, nothing.

The people got closer and yelled to see if I was alright. I pushed my car door open the best I could, unfastened my seatbelt, and stepped out. I fell right on my face.

Dazed and confused on the ground I tried to make sense of what just happened. My thoughts were clouded and jumbled, *'What happened? What have I done?'* Ringing alone in my head without any sort of answer.

I thought I was in some field or ditch someplace until the lights around me started looking familiar. My mind was still so confused.

Finally, I realized I was standing near a parking lot, there were businesses around me, traffic, and people. My mind began to survey the horrific scene. The rental car I drove was strung across the street in shattered pieces. Power lines were hanging down across the street. There was a severed power pole that had crashed through the trees. Power lines were draped all around.

Immediately, fear ripped through my gut. *'Did I kill someone? Was there another car?'*

I was in shock. My mind just stared at the severed telephone pole and the shattered remains of the car I drove, silently resting, smashed. Broken glass, smoke, dust, and the scent of fear.

A wave of relief filled my soul when I discovered there were no other cars involved, only moments after, a wave of fear crashed over me as I saw the gravity of the scene.

I was standing on State Street in one of the busiest intersections in town. So much for the field I thought I was in!

The officers and paramedics checked my vitals, ran tests, and asked the necessary questions. I started shaking uncontrollably. The shock hit my body hard. I maintained the lie that I had no idea what happened.

A police officer told me that they were already in pursuit. They got a call that I was flying through red lights and driving out of control at speeds of sixty miles per hour. The telephone pole helped slow the car down to its final resting place, not before the front end of the car slammed into a tree. The car was totaled while the parking lot and street were covered in broken fragments of the car, downed power lines, and broken tree branches.

I was arrested for drug-induced reckless driving. I professed my innocence but knew they'd find drugs in my system when they sent my blood to the lab. I walked away from that devastating scene virtually unharmed, only a bit shaken up. That annoying seatbelt beep helped to save my life. Without it, I would have surely died.

This was the second near-death experience in the same week! I was beyond out-of-control.

I sat there in the holding cell at the police station with my head hanging limply in my hands, trying to figure out how I was going to explain this to my wife. I didn't even know who I was or what I'd become. When is enough, enough?

Have I Had Enough?

12

'The Rain Came'

"The majority of man's grief comes about through lack of self-control. Self-control is a result of thought-control."

-Napoleon Hill

The following days were filled with a frenzied blur of desperate lies spewing from my mouth, making a futile attempt to explain my actions. At this point, the lies I told were weak and pathetic. I felt like I was clutching and grasping at thin air, everything was slipping from my grasp. There was no truth, I was living one big lie.

I experienced that empty feeling that overwhelms your entire being when you know you've messed up and finally been caught for it. The past week I had managed to nearly kill myself, twice. Bianca understood that somehow these two incidences were connected but I refused to fess up and give her the truth. I stacked lies upon more lies, maniacally intertwined, layer after layer, the lies covered up more lies. She was ready to call it quits.

I had been a father for only six months and I was not acting accordingly. I was out-of-control in every way, and to add insult to injury, I'd just lost another job. All the stress from my deception and lies finally came to a head. Bianca and I got into an argument, pushing her to a point where she just couldn't take it anymore.

During the argument, I looked around at the pictures and plaques hanging on the walls of our home. I knew I was losing my family, briefly glimpsing just how gone I was. For reasons unknown to me, I opened the door and ran outside, not knowing where I was headed, but I left. The wind helped to dry the tears on my face as I headed nowhere. I needed to clear my mind somehow.

I knew I didn't want to lose my family, I knew I messed up, and I knew I was in the clutches of something fiercely powerful. I felt chained in every part of my life. Trapped. A prisoner in my own mind.

I was locked out of living, caged from the inside. Trapped in the web of lies I told, trapped in the friends I chose, trapped in the drug game, trapped under a mountain of debt, all rooted from the confines of my addiction.

While on that walk, I prayed.

I gave my Dad a call and with tears I told him everything I could. He gave me clear advice and counseled me on what to do. He and my step-mom drove out to my neighborhood and picked me up from my walk. I'm sure they could sense that I was on the edge of complete hopelessness. They showed me love and belief in a time when I felt broken, giving me counsel and helping me find a shred of hope.

I felt like I knew what I needed to do. It was time for me to get my family back, time for me to take care of my past, and it was time for me to take control of my future.

I started working with my Dad. He mentored me and worked with me as I started putting the pieces of my life back together. Bianca and I talked, cried together, and agreed to try again. I worked hard with my dad and started distancing myself from some of my old friends.

I felt better about who I was. I remember holding Dominic in my arms at night. I felt like things were finally going to be okay. But even with these miracles going on, I still held on to my little secret. I didn't stop using painkillers. I just couldn't find the willingness or faith to quit. I foolishly held on to that part of my life and all the things that come along with it.

Readily available in my mind I found plenty of excuses and reasons to justify it. The whispers continued, *'I'll stop using after these court cases get resolved. The pills help me be the man people love, I need them, I need them, I need them.'*

Bianca and I were married in May of 2008. I walked down the aisle with my son's hand in mine, he wore a little tuxedo and his eyes were full of so much happiness. The day was filled with excitement and love. But again, those dark storm clouds of my addiction cast a dark and secretive shadow over those bright days.

Two months after our wedding my day of judgement came. I pled guilty for my involvement in the movie theater robbery that occurred in 2002. I had avoided the consequences of that stupid decision for almost six years, and now it was time to finally deal with it.

I felt a ray of relief to finally be taking care of this dark part of my past. I was also sentenced for violating my probation. I had just recently failed a urine test for OxyContin.

When the judge sentenced me to one year in jail I knew the sentence was light in comparison to what it could have been. I think the judge had mercy because it happened six years prior. I remember his last words in the courtroom that day as if they were yesterday, 'Mr. Hiatt, this is your last chance. If you mess this up you're done.'

A few days later I checked into jail. I remember that first night in there, curled in a ball, throwing up, aching, and shivering as the withdrawals from the opiates inched through my body. I thought of my wife and son going to sleep without a husband and without a father. I was gone again, breaking the hearts of all those who care for me.

The physical withdrawals began to subside after a few weeks, but emotionally I was a wreck. I'd been numbing my senses and all my true emotions for so many years and they rushed to the surface quickly. They came upon me like a tidal wave. Tears fell at just the thought of a memory. My past was filled with pain and regret. Even a commercial on television of a father and son playing together brought me to tears. I hid my emotions well, but I was dying on the inside.

A small level of relief came over me knowing I was finally dealing with the carnage from my past. I was blessed to have support and encouragement from my family and from Bianca and her family. They were all so good to me.

Deep down within me I felt a call to awaken my mind and my spirit to something more. Once again, feeling the warrior within me begin to stir.

I wanted to use this experience to become a better man, I knew it was possible, but was I willing to do everything it was going to take? Had the pain stung deep enough?

Have I Had Enough?

13

'Daddy, Where did You Go?'

"The world breaks every one of us, and afterward many are

stronger at the broken places."

-Ernest Hemingway

I entered a thirty-day treatment program, thinking that since I had to be in jail I may as well try and get some help. I enlisted without feeling any reluctance. I knew I was broken and needed help. During the daily groups, I began to learn about addiction. I also experienced a deep and foreboding level of shame for the things I've done. I remember feeling open to what was being discussed but I also felt a strong resistance somewhere in my mind. Almost like an invisible wall was casting a shadow over my understanding, blocking my faith.

I couldn't wrap my mind around some of the change. Maybe there were parts of me that didn't have the willingness to change. I held on tightly to them and turned off my receptiveness.

The beast in the shadows was working overtime in my mind. I remained in a conflicted state. There was a part of me that wanted to do what I knew in my heart to be right, be an honorable son, a great father, and a loving husband. So, why was I having such a hard time committing? Had I just not experienced enough pain? *Had I just not had enough?*

In August of that year I experienced a dose of pain that stung deeper than I'd ever felt before. It was on my son's first birthday. I woke up that morning feeling groggy and disgusted as I lifted my head from the pillow and looked around at where I was. All around me there were guys just as sick as me, lying in their bunks, withdrawing from drugs, and feeling weak and powerless. I looked around at the dingy toilets and the cinderblock walls layered in a dirty, greasy, yellow film. The air smelled of bad breath and piss. The back of my throat filled with bile as I raced to the toilet to puke.

I washed my face off and prepared for group. My thoughts were filled with sadness as I thought about my son, without his dad, on his first birthday. A big celebration was planned, cake, ice-cream, balloons, and surrounded by so many supportive and loving family; but his daddy wasn't there. I was nowhere to be found. It was only his first birthday and I was already bringing confusion to his precious little heart.

During group, we discussed the effects our choices have on all those around us. I remember feeling like the lesson was tailored just for me. God, the master seamstress.

We were asked to take ten minutes to write a letter from someone we hurt in our addiction. The letter was to be from their perspective, aiding us in imagining what it must be like for them.

I chose to write the letter from the perspective of my son, with my non-dominant hand, putting myself in his shoes for a moment. By doing so, I finally began to glimpse a sliver of the pain my life was causing.

Once I finished writing I was asked to stand up and read my letter in front of the class. (I think the instructor could see how emotional I'd become while writing it) So, I stood up and began to read, and by the first word my emotions had rippled past my throat and came crashing out of me. The tears fell down my cheeks as I pictured my baby boy wondering where his daddy could be. I felt my throat seize. I couldn't utter a word, the intensity of the moment gripped my heart and soul. After a moment, I regained my composure and began to read...

Daddy,

Where did you go? I miss you holding me. Do you not love me anymore? If you loved me you would be here with me on my birthday. Come home dad.
Love,

Dominic

As I finished reading the letter there was complete silence in the room. I hurried to my seat feeling broken and lost, finally glimpsing a bit of the madness I'd created. This was the first time my real emotions hit me, for I'd been suppressing them for years.

This was another call to awaken. But how would I choose to answer that call? If I only knew the madness that still lie ahead.

By the time I was finished with treatment I felt like I was ready. Thirty days... of course I'm cured. I remember thinking that if I could just be released from jail all my problems would be solved. I felt good about this newly discovered direction I was headed, but unsure how firm my conviction was. The pain I felt was real, but did it sting deep enough?

Life has a funny way of putting us to the test, especially when we think we have it all figured out.

So, I laid my head down on my bunk that night, staring at the concrete ceiling above.

Have I Had Enough?

14

'The Compromise'

"If you compromise with your conscience it will not be long before you have no conscience. For your conscience will fail to guide you. Just as an alarm clock will fail to waken you if you don't heed it."

-Napoleon Hill

The world turned, along with the hands on the clock mounted on the cinderblock wall, as I lay there on my bunk and watching those hands slowly tick by. Time lapsed symbolic to the dream state, each day seemed eerily similar. I bided my time, never truly being present in the moment. I fortified an invisible wall that blocked off the pathway to change. I felt like I had it all under control, halting my personal growth.

After graduation from treatment I was placed in a privileged section where guys went to work outside of the jail grounds. This setting was more laid-back and I would be faced with more temptations. I was tested within an hour of my arrival.

It was something that, at the time seemed so insignificant. Looking back, I can see clearly how that one seemingly insignificant choice jeopardized the sacred harmony between my conscience and myself, and started me down the pathway of pain.

I was approached by an old friend of mine. He greeted me like old friends do, knowing I was new to the section he welcomed me and helped me feel more comfortable. Then he asked if I wanted a dip. I'd only chewed tobacco once before and I threw up because I was so disgusted by it, but something within me wanted it, something within me *needed* it...

I said yes. Quick as that. No hesitation.

Before long, I was chewing tobacco daily in jail and smuggling cans into the facility. That choice to start chewing created a small crack in my mind, allowing the opposing force to begin chipping away. That one compromise shifted the precious balance in my conscience because it was something I had to lie about.

Along with that compromise came seeds of guilt because I knew in my heart that I wasn't doing everything I could do, to change my behavior. The lies seemed to roll off my tongue a little smoother, the shady me was back. It's not that I lied about chewing tobacco, that question never came up. The problem was that my eyes began to fleet and shift as feelings of guilt began to fill my soul. I was not being true. I created a hole within me because I wasn't being authentic. The hole I felt within got a little bigger with each lie. I listened to the whispers of the opposing force lurking in the shadows of my mind, *'No one will ever know, it's only tobacco, it's not even illegal, you need a head change, you deserve to feel better, numb the pain you feel, you're not hurting anyone, you need this, you need this, you need this.'*

As I fed those thoughts the lies began to flow faster, continually feeding the opposing force and starving the warrior within.

I was so quick to forget.

In the past few months I had almost lost my marriage, my son, and my family while nearly dying because of my choices in addiction. Yet, here I was again, blazing down that same pitiful path.

The stage was being set for another whirlwind of pain, and it all started by that seemingly insignificant compromise. One of the saddest parts is that I was manipulating myself, I believed my lies. I lied to myself under the shifty belief that the guilt I felt was foolish, telling myself that I was in complete control.

After six months, I was released to serve the remaining six months under the supervision of home confinement with an ankle monitor.

Walking out of the cold steel doors of the Jail and into the warm embrace of my wife and precious son felt like heaven. I was home at last.

Since the compromise with tobacco, I had developed a dependency on it, but even more so I'd developed a dependency on lies and manipulation.

Aristotle, profoundly states, "**We are what we repeatedly do.**" I began to discover just how true those words are. I was in the habit of compromising with the guiding light within me and listening to the whispers of the opposing force. That very night I found myself face-to-face with a bottle of alcohol.

While the inviting bottle smiled at me I heard the whispers, *'I'm in control, it's only alcohol, no one will ever know, loosen up, have a little fun, you deserve it, you need it.'*

And in that moment, I believed those whispers and made another compromise because I listened to those seductive thoughts. I tipped my glass back and felt the alcohol warm the back of my throat and down into my stomach. This was the same day I walked out of those cold steel doors of jail. My first day on home confinement and I'd ran into the warm embrace of alcohol. I vividly remember thinking just how in control I was. Now it's clear to see just how out-of-control I'd become.

I got away with it. And I did it again, again, again, and again.

Meanwhile, my little family and I settled into a cozy home on the hillside, and began to build our new life. I worked hard and began to reap some financial rewards. Life was beginning to feel alright. The whispers in my mind continued, *'I finally have it all figured out, I can control my drinking, I need this, I can use, nobody has to know.'*

While on home confinement, we hosted barbecues and get-togethers at our home. I remember watching my son learn and grow. I loved to go on walks with my son, seeing his eyes light up with excitement as he discovered the beauty all around him.

Looking back on that time in my life I am so grateful for those beautiful memories. Life felt perfect. I remember feeling like somehow I was going to be able to hold my little world together. But I still felt the subtle pushes and pulls of the battle within. As I experienced a little more success I became even more cocksure with my choices.

I started drinking alcohol more frequently and smoking cigarettes at work. Then I got more daring, and started taking muscle relaxers and *GHB* because they could fill the hole I felt within and they wouldn't come up on my regular piss tests. All the while I heard the enticing whispers of the opposing force urging me on, *'At least you're not using pain pills, you deserve to have a little fun, you're more fun to be around high, you function better at work high, it's not a big deal, no one will even know, you need this.'* I foolishly believed the lie that *'since I was clean from painkillers, I was in complete control.'*

The environment I worked in was very relaxed and I used work as a place I could party hard. I got hammered at work, passing out on my desk often, while using my drive home to gain my composure before getting home. I'd force a smile as I walked through the door, acting as if all was well.

Very quickly I reached for the harder drugs. I started taking ecstasy regularly, ketamine, and hallucinogenic mushrooms, always washed down with the warm comfort of alcohol. Again, lost in the blinding fog of my addiction. It had only been a year since I stood up in that treatment program and cried as I read the letter from the perspective of my little son, and here I was again, risking my freedom and my life.

I was so quick to forget. When would enough, be enough?

Have I Had Enough?

15

'The Impending Storm'

"The beginning of a habit is like an invisible thread, but every time we repeat the act, we strengthen the strand, add to it another filament, until it becomes a great cable and binds us irrevocably... thought and act."

-Orison Swett Marden

The mental warfare hammered consistently in my mind as I continued to gamble with my life and my freedom. The ploys of that opposing force were subtly, persuasively, and seductively inching me further from the light.

By July of 2009, I was officially released from home confinement. I still don't know how I managed to manipulate my way through those hoops but somehow, I was successful.

With the ankle monitor finally taken off I drove away feeling lighter on my feet, and for the first time in a year, a little taste of freedom. I was excited about the warm summer nights and the freedom to come and go as I pleased. But along with that freedom, I had also strengthened the bonds and chains of my addiction. They were tight and they were heavy. They controlled where I went, what I did, what I felt, and who I was.

My income suffered as I continued to feed my addiction. I felt the stress and financial pressure as I got even further behind on bills. My immediate reaction to stress was resorting to the numbing power of drugs and alcohol. Also, the relationship with my wife became tense, I'm sure she could sense something was going on. I convinced myself that the constant lies and deception where what everyone did. I was living a lie and getting in way over my head, desperately needing a way out.

Then, one day out of the blue, I saw my out. A chance to start a new life, and I took it in a heartbeat. I was offered a job a few thousand miles away in a town just south of Cleveland, Ohio. I took a flight out there to see the operation firsthand. I wanted to get my finger on the pulse of the city and get familiar with the opportunity, and it felt perfect.

The company offered to completely relocate my family, a nice salary with commissions, and huge potential for advancement. I saw it as the perfect opportunity. We were facing financial pressures at home which made this opportunity even more tempting. I also felt like I could just run and escape from the battle I was fighting within, or just get away from all my problems.

I talked it over with my family and agreed to take the job. I was still on probation but had somehow maintained a good relationship with my probation officer. I spoke with him about the job offer and told him my plan to quickly pay off my restitution with the money I made. He seemed a bit hesitant as I related this to him, but he reluctantly agreed to sign a thirty-day travel pass. The pass allowed me to leave Utah for thirty days, during that time I was to check out the job offer, then fly home. If everything was copacetic, he would put together an interstate compact and transfer my probation to Ohio.

Now there's a little point here I'd like to make about habits. When faced with situations or decisions we tend to fall back on our habits, whatever they maybe. By this time, I was in the habit of lying and manipulating, and those habits dominated my life. I continued to lie, and I continued to manipulate. I avoided and shifted responsibility whenever I could, pushing off anything that felt uncomfortable. I shrank from my responsibility to be true to myself. So, naturally, that's how I chose to deal with this situation, and it landed me in deep water.

The company in Ohio agreed to move us out there into a fully furnished condo. They provided everything we needed, under the conditions that I start immediately. I decided to wait until the last possible moment before finally telling my probation officer that I already moved across the country. I hoped it would buy me some time. I lied to my wife by telling her it was all good with probation as I desperately hoped it would all work out. A shady and reckless move on my part.

I nurtured the fear that if I took responsibility and did it the right way, I would lose the opportunity. I didn't want that to happen, so I took the shot and we headed to Ohio.

From day one I felt on top of the world. This was finally it! My new start with my wife and son, just the three of us, and we were finally going to make it. In a new city, making good money, and having the time of our lives. We went shopping, ate at the finest restaurants, and shared quality time as a family; life was perfect.

After a few months, I finally called my probation officer. He was frustrated with me and his frustration turned to vexation as I told him, very nonchalantly, that I had already secured a job and a residence in Ohio. He exclaimed, "You were just supposed to be checking it out, not already moved!" I told him that I was doing better than I'd ever done before so he told me he'd work on filing an emergency compact to transfer my probation, and hopefully get an approval. If not, I'd have to come back.

My lies were crushing me; I could feel it. I was thousands of miles away from home and nobody knew about the trouble I was in with probation. I was in way over my head, and I was lying about it to everyone. To avoid dealing with my feelings I used some kind of inner diversionary trick to continually bury the responsibility and guilt I felt. I buried my fears under a mountain of OxyContin; which, in time, would prove to be my undoing.

I avoided doing anything about my fears. I sought warmth and comfort through alcohol and drugs, desperately hoping that somehow it would all just go away.

Meanwhile, my family and I were enjoying a glimpse of the finer things in life. We took our son to watch the *Cleveland Browns* play during Monday Night Football. We even sat close to the court and watched *LeBron James* lead the *Cavaliers*.

We danced, we laughed, and we lived it up. It was some of the best times of my life but I knew that one day soon it would all be over, and I hated that reality. I wished I could just freeze time.

Work continued to go extremely well, as I worked hard I rose quickly to the top. Before long I was promoted to floor manager, working directly with the owners and had my hand in overseeing all the leaders, staff, and the company sales. I felt like I was in my element, I felt alive, and for the first time in my life I truly felt accomplished. I was living my dream and it just kept getting better. It was a dream I didn't want to wake up from.

But, as they say, *'pride comes before the fall.'* I was beginning to feel untouchable, it was only a matter of time before I fell.

I began drinking heavily at work. The guys I worked with partied hard and we all had some big egos. After work we'd stroll the night streets of Cleveland like we were royalty. Masked by ego, I was dying inside and my addiction to painkillers was taking on a life of its own.

The season began to change as the cold winter snow blanketed the town. With the feelings of Christmas in the air, we boarded our plane to fly home for the holiday. Life was going so good, on the outside. I was on top of the world traveling with my family and feeling the taste of some financial success.

As the plane touched down in Utah I felt a sense of comfort, it felt good to be home. We shared time with our families for Christmas and I remember thinking that everything felt perfect in that moment. I had thoughts of checking in with my probation officer, even lying to myself that I would. But I knew if I went to see him there was a good chance I was going to jail, and I didn't want to lose it all.

Instead I listened to those enticing whispers of the opposing force, *'You're in control, nobody needs to know, you're doing the right thing by not telling anyone, you need this, once you take a pill everything will be okay.'*

So, I picked up fifty *Roxicodone* (each pill contained thirty milligrams of potent painkiller) and immediately sniffed two of them. In that moment, all my fears went away and I was up in the clouds again. I knew one day I was going to fall, but I didn't want to fall just yet.

My wife, our little son and I flew back to Ohio after Christmas. I didn't end up calling my probation officer, all I managed to do while we were there was call my drug dealer, so I flew back in the middle of a full-blown relapse. I understood that all my chips were in now and the storm clouds grew darker by the minute.

In January of 2010, I finally made the dreaded call to my probation officer. His first words were, "Ahhhh, there you are!" and by his tone I knew I was in for it. I quickly filled the air with a flustered ramble, desperately scrambling to relay all the good things happening in my life. Then I started with all the lies. I told him I was clean, sober, and doing better than I've ever done before. Then the line was silent. He let the silence hang in the air for a very uncomfortable minute, until I heard his frustrated exhale, followed by the bombshell...

"Ryan, I understand you've been doing good and that's encouraging, but you've left me no choice. My hands are tied, you've got a warrant out for your arrest.

Have I Had Enough?

16

'Secrets and Lies'

"Character is a quality that embodies many important traits such as integrity, courage, perseverance, confidence, and wisdom. Unlike your fingerprints that you were born with and can't change, character is something that you create within yourself and must take responsibility for changing."

-Jim Rohn

I felt a crushing weight slam my body as soon as my probation officer expressed those words. It all seemed final, I knew I was done for. My ears barely heard the rest of what he said. Panic and fear coursed through me. When he spoke, it was as if an explosion had just gone off and my ears were still ringing from the noise. Then I felt a humbling wave of desperation.

I attempted to maintain my composure on the phone but I'm sure I sounded so distant. Quickly I expressed a desperate plan to save up some money, pay off my restitution, and move my family back to Utah.

My hope was that by paying off my restitution it would help to sway the judge's decision. I hung up the phone with my probation officer and quickly reached into my pocket to the warm comfort of painkillers.

Then I lost it, like a dog off his chain, out of control.

I spiraled down, faster and darker than ever before. I reached to the numbing power of OxyContin and started using thousands of dollars' worth every week. The temporary numbing effect was merely a bi-product to what happened as I complicated every problem I was faced with. I chose to keep the warrant to myself, went to work, put the blinders on, and buried myself in painkillers, hoping to somehow escape the reality I was living in. I worked harder and harder, making more and more money; consequently, spending more and more on painkillers. I was using over three-hundred milligrams per day; enough to kill someone, easily.

Most mornings I would snort an eighty milligram OxyContin, then climb back into bed so the pain would go away. Then, on my way to work I would chug an energy beer. All of this was before work at eight-thirty in the morning. I was the first one there and I was lit by the time anyone else arrived.

I was always reaching for something to make me feel better. Filled with an insatiable thirst and desperate hunger for the feeling of my drugs, and the feelings they helped me to block out.

Nicotine was a constant for me, always flowing through my veins. I chewed *Copenhagen* when I was indoors and I smoked *Marlboro* lights when I was outdoors. I even started using sniffing tobacco. I was a total wreck.

So, there I stood in those cold winter months of Ohio. I was dressed in a crisp suit, a designer p-coat, a scarf draped loosely around my neck, and it all came together with the shine of cuff-links and the nicest tie money could buy. I looked like a million bucks. I was the man with it all together. On the outside, I had it all. I was experiencing small tastes of financial success that afforded me the look of 'the man with it all together.' Only this 'man with it all together' was living a double life. He was dying inside. His life was anything but together.

To paint the contrast is stark. It's depressing now as I think of some of the other titles befitting me. A fugitive from justice, an alcoholic, a drug addict, liar, fraud, wanted by the U.S. Marshals, a man hopelessly lost, and scared. Those are just a few of the titles that could rightfully be placed on this 'man with it all together.'

I lied to cover up more lies, always attempting to put a good face on my life. But, if you looked close enough, in the creases under my eyes you could see glimpses of the guilt I felt. I was hiding so much from my family and all those who cared for me, and the guilt I felt began to weigh heavily. I knew what I was doing was wrong, but I didn't stop.

As my addiction grew, the thoughts from the opposing force raged in my mind, *"You're in control, you're providing for your family, it's better if your wife doesn't know, you're saving her from heartache, deal with it later, it will be easier then, just another pill, you'll feel better, you need it, you need me.'*

I just wanted to freeze time and run away from the hell I was living in, all at the same time.

To put a band-aid on the chaos I began spending excessively. I splurged at the malls and the clubs downtown. Every time I bought something I felt a little better, but it went away so quickly and I was left feeling more empty than before.

The days turned into months and I continually avoided any responsibility to deal with my warrant. I was a slave to pain pills, day after day, pill after pill, lie after lie. I remember the feeling I experienced every night when I made it home from work. I loved walking in my door and seeing love and recognition in Dominic's eyes. He would jump up from his toys and run to me with his hands up exclaiming, "Daddy!" And I'd breathe the ultimate sigh of relief, for I'd made it, one more day. I felt so safe as he ran into my arms. I felt peace.

Those moments are such tender memories, even as I think of them now. He is a special boy. He means everything to me. But in the dusty recesses of my mind the hurricane I was creating was gaining momentum and it was only a matter of time before it hit, and I knew it was doomed to cause his heart so much pain.

By that time, I was using around two-thousand dollars' worth of pain pills every week. As my income increased, so did my drug use.

I was living for the moment while in a constant state of fear that each day would be my last, staring at the world through my rearview mirror. I just kept pushing, kept running, and knew all along that the law was getting closer. I was running from everything, running from the truth, running from the future, running from my past, running from the old me, running from the law, running from responsibility...and I just couldn't stop running.

Then things changed drastically...

The owners of the company came up to my office and shut the door. I could tell this was something serious. To make a long story short, they told me they opted to sell the company, as of today, all operations ceased. They sold the company, right out from under us. All the risk, all the hard work, done. And to make matters worse, I had to go tell the company they were all out of a job. Frustration and confusion filled my heart as I realized the proverbial bottom had just fallen out. Now what?

I took the opportunity to move my family back home. I knew I needed to prepare to face my past. One of the biggest fears I had while living in Ohio was being arrested in front of my family. In a way, I felt relieved that we were headed home. Feelings of scarcity began to fill my soul and I needed some time to think. I decided to fly Bianca and Dominic back home immediately while I stayed to pack up our home and close everything out. As the boxes piled up I felt an exhausting weight around me. Each box held memories of what could have been, and I knew things would never be the same.

As I finished boxing everything up my soul was discouraged and jaded. I felt like giving up on life. I sat there in my home, surrounded by boxed memories and feelings of emptiness, while inside I was encompassed by guilt, fear, and shame. I was defeated. My mind filled with an overwhelming helplessness. I felt like I had let everyone around me down. It's impossible to describe the emptiness I felt, within. There was a part of me that didn't want to live anymore.

Filled with regret, I sat alone on my couch with my eyes locked on the pills scattered on the glass coffee table.

As if it were a ritualistic trance, I stripped the time release coating off the Oxy, crushed it up into a fine powder, and scooped it with my card into a line on the table. Then I crushed another and then another. The pile of finely crushed Oxy moved my stomach to knots. I rolled up a twenty-dollar bill and sniffed as hard as I could, instantly blasting the drug up my nose. The comfort, the numb, the warmth... I was okay again.

The world turned and time slowly ticked by while I stared out the window of our home. I was still surrounded by boxes and memories, but inside I felt empty, defeated, and tired. All I could do was sit there, for hours, smoking and nodding off while my mind filled with fear and hopelessness. I felt nauseous, but for the moment I was where I wanted to be, escaping real life and any responsibility. But I knew it would be short lived. I knew my day of reckoning was rapidly approaching.

I wanted to freeze time, but completely escape the moment... I was lost.

Have I Had Enough?

17

'Hanging by a Moment'

"Fear causes hesitation, and hesitation causes your worst fears to come true."
-Patrick Swayze

(Point Break film)

The movers picked up our belongings and I headed to the airport to catch a flight home. It was over, my brief respite to Ohio had come to an end, and I was in horrible shape, much worse than when I left.

I gazed despairingly out the window as the airplane headed toward *Salt Lake International Airport*. I remember watching Cleveland disappear beneath me. My little dream was over and I was flying back to my past.

As I touched down in Utah I half expected the U.S. Marshals to be there with handcuffs. I felt relief as I walked through the airport without a hitch.

Bianca's loving parents opened their doors to us until we got back on our feet. They embraced me like a son. I felt defeated within, knowing I had so many great people who believed in me and were pulling for me, but also knowing that inside I was a fraud.

The frustration grew even more as I began to realize how big of a mess I'd gotten my family into. I held on to so many secrets and lies all while I was on the continual hunt to numb reality. I could tell Bianca was worried. I'm sure she could feel my anxiety and tell something was wrong, being married to an addict like me.

A few weeks later we decided to drive down to Las Vegas and celebrate our anniversary. We relaxed by the pool, ate well, and danced the night away. For a moment things felt perfect again. I didn't want our vacation to end.

A police cruiser got behind us on the drive home. My heart started beating so fast as I focused on the road and checked my speed. He just cruised behind me for a while. I thought for sure this was the moment I'd been dreading for so long. After what seemed like an eternity, he finally clicked on his blinker and drove past us. My heartbeat eventually slowed and we continued home. Just another reminder of how divided my life had become. That type of thing happened so often. I knew one day soon my luck would run out.

Because of my efforts in Ohio I was offered a floor manager position for a company in Salt Lake City. I saw it as a good opportunity to get ahead and hopefully, somehow, deal with the problems I'd created. We rented a condo on the hillside, sitting ironically on the outskirts of the Utah State Prison.

As work prospered I continually fed my addiction. It was like I never missed a beat. The thoughts I had of saving money and dealing with my warrant were buried deeper and deeper in my mind. I just kept pushing off responsibility, telling myself I'd come clean to my wife after our anniversary, then after the Fourth of July, then after her birthday, then after Dominic's birthday, then after Thanksgiving...

'When it comes to making changes, tomorrow never comes.'

...and tomorrow never came. Thanksgiving turned into Christmas and I never took the time. I was lost in my addiction, experiencing close call after close call, as I tiptoed the line of life and death.

I felt like I was clawing at thin air... and I just kept falling.

The walls were closing in on me. On my way to work I happened across a wanted picture of me in *Busted* magazine. I knew it was only a matter of time until I was caught.

I couldn't get myself to surrender. In my mind, it wasn't an option, there was no way I was going to take responsibility. I just ran, hid, lied, and pushed it all off. I knew one day it would all come crumbling down.

One night I remember nodding out at home, as Bianca grabbed me by the shirt I could see worry and fear in her eyes. She told me she couldn't stand to see me like this anymore, and asked what I was hiding from her. I wonder what she saw in my eyes?

I almost spilled everything to her that night. I wanted to so bad! I wanted to just unload it all to her. I wanted to be true. For all I was putting her through she deserved the truth, but I just couldn't get myself to do it.

I continued to lie, and lie, and lie, like a pathetic sap, I never took the time. I was living so many lies that I didn't know who I was anymore. The law closing in on me, the weight of my choices crushing down on me, and I was trying desperately to escape it all. There were times I wished my life would end.

I quit my job in Salt Lake City and started flying to Boise to work on the weekdays and I'd fly home for the weekends. I was scattered and scrambling trying desperately to hold on to my fragile world. The bills stacked up and I felt swamped in debt, while the discontent in my home was all amplified and suffering at the hands of my addiction.

I remember sitting on my back porch and inhaling the smoke from my cigarette. As the smoke inched out of my mouth and filled my view I glanced at the grounds of the Utah State Prison. Part of me knew that was where I was headed.

My pride, ego, and an intrinsic selfishness were fueled by my addiction to pain pills. I just wasn't willing to humble myself and come clean to the lies. I was hanging by a moment, waiting for it all to come crashing down.

I lived each day in the shadow of fear, reaching quickly to numb the shame I felt. I was tangled in a web of lies and deceit. I was wearing down myself and all those around me. Every corner, every turn, every sunrise, and every sunset I thought would be my last. As I lay in bed each night I half expected the doors to be kicked in. I'd wake up from nightmares where the swat team dropped in my windows from ropes and arrested me.

Fear ruled every waking hour, even when I slept.

Holidays turned into birthdays and finally to a new year. I never took the time to come clean to my family. All the while I scraped to feed my addiction. I bounced from job to job, experiencing brief success followed by devastating failure, every time. My addiction controlled my destiny at that point.

In March of 2011, I was celebrating my twenty-ninth birthday. I was at work and I pushed the limits again. It had become such a common thing for me to do. I overdosed at the office, causing a scene as I was carried out by some work buddies. I regained consciousness later that night and crept in my home past midnight. I was gone for my own birthday, choosing drugs over my family. I broke Bianca's heart more and more every day. It was only a matter of time before I was found out.

Days turned into weeks as I felt the storm rapidly approaching.

Each night I would kiss my son on the forehead and tuck him into bed. I wanted to shield him from the storm that was at our doorstep. I wanted it with all my heart, but my mind was ruled by my addiction and I just couldn't stop the madness... the opposing force had a powerful grip on my mind.

My fears were closing in...

Have I Had Enough?

18

'Beneath the Bright Lights'

"Things which matter most should never be at the mercy

of things which matter least."

-Johann Von Goethe

I came home from work early on a Monday night in April 2011. Bianca had planned pizza and a family night. She always did such an amazing job bringing our family together, even as I was tearing it apart. The mood that evening was light and fun. Dominic was full of energy and happiness as he ran around our home in his Batman pajamas. He sang and danced and laughed at the top of his lungs.

The three of us were experiencing one of those blessed moments as a family where things just felt perfect. That perfect moment is one I'll always hold dear to me because in the next moment my whole little world came crumbling down.

I heard my phone ring and as I went to answer it I had to catch my breath, I was winded from chasing Dominic around the living room.

I answered the phone in a ramble of laughter while asking him if he got the email I sent. Only silence came from the other end of the phone. Finally, the awkward silence snapped me out of it. I could feel something was wrong so I asked what it was. He took a solemn breath and said, "Bad news Ryan." He related to me that a friend of his had seen a preview of tonight's ten o'clock news, and my face was going to be on it, as a wanted fugitive.

My heart dropped like a ton of bricks crushing through a glass dome, my little world shattered. I was speechless, all the laughter in the room faded from my clouded mind, alone in my thoughts I knew this was it. My time was finally up. I knew it was over. I held on to one last glimmer of desperate hope that somehow this was all just a big mistake, but deep down I knew my day was here. I'd been running too long. I'd been on the run for almost two years and all I managed to do was back myself deeper into a corner, leaving my family at the mercy of it.

As the night wound down Bianca took our son up to bed. *Batman* reluctantly grabbed her hand and marched up to bed, I could tell he didn't want the night to end either. As my little superhero and his mom walked to his room I bent down and hugged them both tightly, knowing that things would never be the same again. I went downstairs and sat there, alone on the couch, staring blankly at the television as the ten o'clock new aired. I felt paralyzed, sitting there waiting, wishing, and hoping that it was all just a mistake. But I knew my time was up.

Then it happened.

My face, plastered on our television, could've been as big as life itself. The caption read: ***Wanted fugitive; Ryan David Hiatt.*** Along with the caption was a list of my haunting rap-sheet.

There I was. That's him. That's the guy. The man I'd been running from for all these years, was staring right back at me. The hourglass was empty, my time was up.

As the world turned, my stomach tied in knots. All the deception, all the lies, all the fear, all the stress, all the worry, and all those sleepless nights; all of it came crashing down. I just sat there stunned on the couch.

The world seemed to slow and then finally, time stood still.

Everything I'd been running from for all those years was finally here, on display for the world to see. I lived in fear of this moment but had created no actual plan for it. I paced my living room and figured I only had ten minutes or so before the task force arrived. Lots of people knew where I lived, it's not like it was a secret.

Finally, I snapped out of the shock and ran upstairs. With a look of bewilderment in my eyes I exclaimed, "B, we gotta go, now! Two minutes' tops! Grab your bags, clothes, and everything you'll need for a few days. I'll go get Dom." I'm sure she could see the panic in my eyes. She looked shocked, worried, and just plain confused. "What!? Why? What's going on Ryan? Tell me what happened?" And with all the strength I could muster I remarked with a defeated tone, "I can't tell you right now, there's no time. We've got to go."

I woke up Dom and told him we were going on a car ride. He jumped into my arms with a smile on his face. *Batman* loves car rides. I scanned my room, grabbed what I could, and headed for the door.

Before closing the door behind me I took one last look at our home. I knew I would never see it again. I knew things would never be the same. I shut the door and ran to the car, started it up, and sped away with my family.

The following two weeks are a bittersweet blur of misery and heartache. Concerned family and friends called as the news spread like wildfire. We holed up in a secluded hotel get-away near Park City. I broke my wife's heart, piece by piece, as I told her little fragments of the truth always laced with sugar cubes, lies to help make it all go down a little smoother.

My secret was finally out in the open, but I persisted with lies that aimed to shift responsibility and make me the good guy. I held on to my own little secret. The severity of my addiction was guarded tightly within me. It was locked away, in the safe within the safe, and I wasn't about to let go of my stronghold.

I tried to stay calm as the storm was upon us. We went to the movies as a family and went out to eat, but the tension was getting tighter by the minute. On Easter Sunday, we attended an Easter egg hunt at the hotel. I remember watching my son run around and pick up treats, it brought a smile to my face even as I was dying inside.

I stood there and thought about the choices in front of me, I knew what I had to do. I was tired, tired of running, tired of lying, and tired of the fight. I needed to turn myself in.

I've been blessed in my life to have a mother with an unwavering belief in me. I told her of my plans and she said, "No matter what happens my son, embrace this journey ahead, use it for good, to better your life, and all those along your path. Share your journey of strength and of the warrior you have within you."

I'm grateful today for those words and the belief she shared behind them, the power of her suggestion has guided me along my path.

I planned to head to the jail the following day. Dominic and I had a sleepover that night, every time I looked into his loving eyes my heart tied up in knots. We built a fort with couches that night and played until his eyes got heavy and he fell asleep in the nook of my arm. I held my little superhero in my arms and watched him fall asleep. I remember feeling his heart beat next to mine and thinking of the devastation and hurt I was about to cause him. I lay there feeling nervous for what the future held. So, I held my son and wished that moment would never end.

But, the morning inevitably came. I said heartfelt goodbyes to my family as they each gave me their blessing. With every goodbye, I saw glimpses into the pain I caused them.

Me, my son, and my wife got into our car and headed off. Dominic was in the backseat, and as I watched his eyes through the rear-view mirror I could tell he knew something wasn't right. Something was going on between his mom and dad.

We stopped off at her parents' home to drop off our son before we headed to the jail. I stood alone at the corner of the house and watched as Dominic ran around the backyard. It all seems slow motion to me now, a moment frozen in time.

I watched the beautiful smile on his face, I saw the summer wind blow his hair, and I can still hear his tender laugh. Happiness, such a novel idea, and I saw it in his eyes. Pure and unadulterated happiness. With not a care in the world, his smile resembled all the joy that's in it.

I stood there and watched him play for a while until I finally walked up to him and caught him in my arms. I knelt to him and hugged him with all the strength and love I could muster.

He is my star. My sunshine. My little buckaroo. My superhero. My son...and he held me with all the love and strength of the world that day. I melted in his little arms.

That little three-year old boy held up his broken dad, and gave me the courage to go on. As he held me I whispered to him, "I love you my son, always remember that okay buddy? I'm going away for a while. I'm going to do everything possible to make it count. I love you. Goodbye son."

A lifetime worth of tears pooled up in a place deep within me as he said, "Okay daddy, I love you."

I stood there and watched him run off to play, and that moment is seared into the depths of my heart forever. Words can't describe the pain I felt in that moment.

As my wife and I pulled up to the jail, the feeling was tense and stressed. I saw goodbye in her eyes as she drove off. I knew it. I'd caused her way too much pain and shattered her heart.

I stood there alone in the jail parking lot and watched her drive away. It was just me now and the doors to the jail in the distance. Occasionally I would glance toward those doors, they seemed so daunting. I knew I had a long road ahead, but I was ready, I was so tired, I'd been running from myself for far too long, I'd been running from my past and running from my truth. I ran from everything for far too long.

I had pain pills coursing through my veins and I knew the pending withdrawal from them would be nasty. But part of me felt so worn, beaten, and tired that I just didn't care anymore. I felt the weight lift off my shoulders as I walked toward the entrance of the jail. The man from my past finally joined the man of today, and as one I walked up to those giant steel doors. With one last sigh of defeat I notified the authorities who I was and that they were looking for me.

They popped the door and I stepped inside. Then I looked up to the concrete and steel that surrounded me. This was going to be a long ride. Very quickly I felt a chill pierce my bones as I heard those cold steel doors click shut behind me.

Have I Had Enough?

Part II

'Awakening

the

Warrior Within'

19

'On a Bus Bound for Prison'

"I could be thankful even for this awful illness...cunning, baffling and powerful. That has taught me to weep and to mourn and to laugh out loud and better and for real. And thankful that, of all the fatal diseases my son might have gotten, he got the one where there is this little sliver of hope that if he surrenders he'll survive."
-Thomas Lynch
(on his child's addiction)

Two weeks after those steel doors clicked shut behind me, I was sitting on a bus bound for prison. The eerie rattling from the shackles and chains around my ankles and wrists caused a shutter up my spine. These chains reminded me of the shackles of my addiction that I'd worn for so long. As the bus headed towards the prison I reflected on the past two weeks, still shocked from what had all happened.

The judge wasted no time with his decision. It was clear and concise. He spoke of the countless lies and manipulations I must have used as I paraded my family around the country, while unbeknownst to them, I was a wanted fugitive and hopelessly addicted.

He spoke of my blatant disregard for the rules of society. I'd left him no choice. It was finally my time to pay the price. I was sentenced to serve up to fifteen years in the Utah State Prison.

I felt numb as those words escaped the judges mouth. Dazed and in shock I trailed the bailiff as he escorted me toward the exit of the courtroom. It all felt surreal to me as I made one final glance back and saw tears falling from the eyes of my wife. That heartbroken image is the last thing I saw before the door to the courtroom closed shut behind me.

Immediately I was placed in the confines of a solitary holding cell. It was just me, the shackles, the chains, and the concrete. I felt the weight of the world upon me as my body collapsed to the floor, curling up in a ball of hopelessness. I'd resisted the outcome of my reality for far too long, and now, I was trapped in the devastating reality I'd created. My soul was racked with guilt and despair as I buried my head in my hands and thought, 'What have I done?'

Chugging along the freeway in that bus bound for prison my eyes held the glazed look of a man defeated and broken. Staring out the window I watched as so many familiar places whizzed past. My mind sparkled with fading memories as my soul harrowed up the guilt.

The prison bus finally slowed to exit the freeway and came to a stop at the intersection. A right turn and a few blocks up the road to the east was my home, my wife, and my precious son. My family was so close, yet so far away.

But we weren't headed that way, the bus turned west and sputtered its way to the prison. We rounded the corner and inched our way toward the gate. Passing under razor-wire layered with more razor-wire, my eyes glimpsed the towers, yards, and fences that covered the vast complex. My body felt a chill to the core as I looked at this relic of a prison.

I felt engulfed by a deep foreboding as I looked up to the towering structures. I felt like I was going to throw up as my stomach tensed and churned. Then the bus slowed to a stop. I didn't want to get up, but it was time for me to go. As I stood up I could hear the clink and clank of the shackles and chains. I finally stepped off the bus while the chains continued to ring on the concrete. Finally, my eyes looked around and took in the oppressing view. I was about to enter the grounds of the Utah State Prison, and I was in way over my head.

When I was just a young boy my family and I would drive north to grandpa and grandma's house. We made that trip to Salt Lake City every few Sundays. They lived only an hour away from us but that drive felt like such a long adventure when I was young. My grandpa and grandma are so special to me. They will always be my heroes.

We would share time together and sit down to eat grandma's homemade Sunday dinner. I can still smell the fresh dinner rolls in the kitchen, and taste the ice-cream she served in a little glass bowl.

During the car ride, my brothers, sister, and I would fill the car with imagination, always fueled by moms intriguing questions. Without fail we would drive past the prison, sitting just off the side of the interstate. As we drove past I remember feeling the daunting energy around it, it felt so heavy to me even as a young boy. It held a dark mystery behind it, and I knew as a young lad that it was a place to stay away from. My imagination created a detailed image of what it must be like, behind those fences and walls.

And here I stood, some twenty years later, shackled, chained, and preparing to enter the front gate. As those towers loomed over me I felt smaller than I've ever felt before. Maybe it was the choices from my past and the weight of guilt I felt towering over me, whatever it was, my reality hit me hard.

Constricted by the chains I hobbled closer to the entrance. The clang of the metal on the concrete seemed to drown out the voices around me, as time stood still in my mind. I felt hopelessly lost. I was about to enter the front gates of the prison, wishing with everything in me that I could somehow wake up from this nightmare. I wished I could be home with my family, but I knew that wish wouldn't be coming true any time soon.

I walked up to the gate and looked toward the massive prison complex. My mind was unable to fully comprehend the horror of the reality I was living in.

The armed guards ushered me inside the prison gates and escorted me down a maze of entrances and hallways. The paint and grime along the walls told a story of decades of despair. That prison was corroded and hardened.

With a passive resignation, I began to strip off my clothes, shoes, and the last of my possessions. I was down to nothing, and that frightened me.

I stood there naked against the wall, stripped of everything external. I felt uncomfortable, bare, and more insignificant than I ever thought possible. Then I put on the uniform. It was an orange jumpsuit with the words UDC Inmate written down the legs and across the top. I slid on the blue shoes, sat down, and buried my head in my hands.

After placing all my clothes into a small cardboard box, I walked towards the wall to pose for my mugshot. Incomprehensible demoralization at its finest.

I remember looking down at my naked ring finger. I could feel the weight as if my ring were still around my finger. Although my wedding band was gone, I could still feel the weight of living a lie, the weight of neglected responsibility, the weight of guilt crushing down on me, and the weight of my past choices bearing down on my heart and mind. And all that weight was summed up by the significance of a ring, no longer there.

As I was escorted down the narrow hallway I looked up to the ceiling, it seemed to extend forever. The old concrete was cracked from the years, while the layers of chipped paint told the age.

I could feel a consuming cold emanating from the steel bars. The noise, voices, yelling, and screaming were incessant, almost suffocating. I couldn't even tell where it was all coming from. The hoopla was a constant hum that echoed through the bars. The yelling and banging and clinking of steel was overbearing. I felt the noise and energy vibrate to my core. My heartbeat quickened as my mind crept closer to the edge.

The prison guard told me my cell number so I took a right and stepped inside. The steel bars slammed shut behind me with a rickety bang. Although I could hear what sounded like thousands of people yelling and screaming all around me, I felt alone.

I paced to the back of my cell, turned around, and then slowly walked back up to the bars. My hands wrapped around the cold bars of my prison cell as I looked out to the prison I was in. My mind recalled the picture of what I had imagined this place was like so many years ago, and that horrid imagination I had as a young boy twenty years earlier couldn't have been more precise.

There I was. Prison. I'd officially made it, the low of the low.

Have I Had Enough?

20

'I Cannot do This Alone'

"Deep within humans dwell those slumbering powers; powers that would astonish them, that they never dreamed of possessing; forces that would revolutionize their lives if aroused and put into action."
-Orison Swett Marden

I found myself sitting on a rusty old bunk, caught in awe, as I surveyed the cell surrounding me. The aged concrete walls were sparsely covered in sixty years' worth of decaying paint. The walls and ceiling were covered in faded writings from the souls who had come before me. The untold stories behind those writings could serve to define the meaning of hopelessly lost, but I read others that defined the meaning of hope. It was an astonishing contrast.

The walls were dimly lit by a flickering light, barely illuminating the cast-iron sink basin. I couldn't find the courage to even look at the toilet yet. The section I was housed in was, at one time, used as death row. I could feel a heavy energy there.

All my senses were extremely hypersensitive, even the cell felt extra cold. I could feel the cold bite deep into my bones. The yelling and screaming grew louder and louder. As my vision focused I began to see every little daunting detail around me.

My mind went a million places at once, rehashing a lifetime of choices. Finally, as the twilight hours passed, the incessant noise began to fade. Unfortunately, the noise from my thoughts continued to pound my brain.

As I laid there, staring up at the ceiling, I felt my mind slip in and out of consciousness. I was dreaming, then waking, then wishing I was only dreaming. After what felt like an eternity, I heard the sounds of morning. There were no windows so I was aware only by the song of birds as they chirped and nested in the walls of that broken prison. The chirping in the stillness of the morning brought a feeling of tranquility, but that moment of peace was short-lived.

Moments later I began feeling disoriented and lost. I was unsure what this new day had in store for me, which instantly created a mind full of hopeless thoughts and a frenzied panic. The mountain I had ahead of me felt insurmountable. I didn't think I had it in me to go on another step.

Worry and fear filled my thoughts, 'How long am I going to be imprisoned? Is my marriage going to last? How is Dominic going to feel? He lost his daddy and I broke his heart. Will he hate me for what I've done? AAHHHHH, what have I done!?'

I just wanted to curl into a ball and die. I wanted to run and escape it all, but I was trapped. A prisoner of my mind and locked in a prison cell. The depth of hopelessness I felt created a new pathway within my mind, a seed of understanding and awakening that told me, '**I cannot do this alone.**' As I laid there in that prison cell the seeds of this new understanding began to grow.

Meanwhile, the withdrawal effects from the pain pills began to subside, at least physically. My body still ached but I was beginning to feel a little better because the puking had become less frequent. Emotionally I was a complete wreck though. Like the tides of the ocean my emotions crashed down constantly on me. I felt hopeless.

My thoughts consumed me as their negative nature drained the life and spirit out of me. I felt beaten and broken. By this time the others were awake and they sounded like a crazed army yelling and screaming, a constant echo permeating through the concrete and steel.

The hell I created in my mind had now manifested in my surroundings. I was imprisoned in my mind while physically trapped in my prison cell.

After a few hours, I was allowed out of my cell for a few minutes to shower. I walked quickly past the other cells and stepped into the small concrete room they called a shower. Three sides were moldy concrete and the fourth side was wide open. With each unsure step, I felt more and more nauseous. The ground and walls were covered in a thick film of mildew, mold, and who knows what else. In disgust, I almost turned around, but instead I tiptoed on my sandals and pushed the shower button. Now, I'm over six feet tall, the shower head was installed at about four feet high. I'm sure you get the picture.

I tried my best to block out everything around me. It's safe to say that was the quickest shower of my life. To make matters worse, someone flushed the toilet and it immediately caused scorching hot water to hit me. I guess it was faulty plumbing in that old prison. I quickly dried off and ran back to my cell feeling dirtier and more frustrated than when I left.

The following days ticked by, alone in my thoughts, filled with doubt and despair. After about a week, I was told to roll up my stuff because I was being moved to another section. As I stepped past the bars of that rickety old cell I was immediately shackled and escorted with a line of other convicts. Shouts and screams pervaded from the cells as we slowly walked past them.

Finally, we made it to a door and walked outside. The warm sunshine blinded me temporarily but it felt so rejuvenating on my skin. Warmth and light; I was unsure if these things still existed. As my eyes focused I took in my surroundings. I saw the guard towers connected by layers and rows of razor wire and fence. Then I saw the concrete and cinderblock buildings all around me. As the shackles clanked across the pavement I remember wondering just where I was going next.

As we continued walking, I glanced southeast toward the Rocky Mountains. I could see my neighborhood. Not long before, I was sitting on my back porch and looking down at these same prison grounds, now here I stood. I thought of my home, my wife, and my precious son. 'What have I done?'

We continued walking until we entered a cinderblock building, as I stood there I was overcome by yelling from the others souls, caged in cells all around me. It sounded like the echo and noise from an indoor pool filled with hundreds of people. The sickness I felt in my stomach consumed me as I was escorted to my cell on the top tier. I entered a cell equipped with a stainless-steel toilet, sink, and an upper and lower bunk. There was a little sliver of a window that faced the east. I was locked in there for twenty-three hours a day, the hour I was let out to shower was between five and six a.m. My cellmate looked as sick as I felt. We were just two men who had lost our way.

My body reached a point of utter exhaustion that night, finally even my mind was too tired to think. So, that night I got some much needed rest. By five o'clock in the morning I mustered the determination to shower. It was a close second to how quick the last one was. Once again, the grossest shower I've ever seen.

During the following days and nights, thoughts of a more positive nature began surfacing in my mind. I remember thinking, 'I want to live. I want to be free. I'm tired of this way of life. I know I can't do it alone.' And with each of those thoughts I began to feel the warrior within me awakening.

In the early morning hour, I watched the magnificent sun slowly rise above the mountain. As the sun inched its way up my heart inched its way open. From the solitude of that prison cell I watched sun rise and I prayed. It was a prayer of surrender. I knew, with every fiber of my being, that I couldn't do it on my own. I needed help, and in that moment, I distinctly remember feeling comforted and loved.

Have I Had Enough?

21

'Be the Man You Want to Be'

"A time comes when you need to stop waiting for the man you want to become and start being the man you want to be."
                                                            -Bruce Springsteen

From the confines of my prison cell, the minutes slowly turned to hours, and I began to experience an awakening within the depths of my soul. Along with that awakening I felt a pain so deep it seared the heart of my soul. It woke me to the point of near panic. I felt a burning desire from the depths of my being to change my life.

In that moment, it's as if my eyes were opened and I saw clearly where each path led.

The pain finally stung deep enough.

But I'd wanted a better life before, only to go back to my old ways. I'd wanted to stop using pills before, only to go back. I remember wanting to stop drinking, wanting to stop lying, wanting to be trusted, honorable, and seen for who I truly am. So, what makes this time any different?

It was time for me to make a choice. I remembered the promise I made to my son, I felt the warrior within me rising to stand tall, and I felt ready to finally stand and face what was in front of me. I felt a bit nervous and unsure about what was next, but within me I felt the desire, and a seed of faith that it was possible.

"You are limited only by the depth of your desire."
-Napoleon Hill

About a month later an officer came over the speaker and told me to rollup. I had no clue where I was headed, or what was next, but I quickly got my things ready and walked out of my cell. I was shackled and escorted through a maze of hallways until finally being placed inside another holding cell. After what seemed like hours I was loaded into a transport van. The armed driver said we were being transferred but couldn't tell us where. So, we drove away. I was shackled and chained in a prison van headed south and my mind created a million possibilities.

As I stared out the window to the east I watched the morning sun light up the valley. We drove on I-15 and as we passed that solemn spot on the side of the interstate where I had almost died ten years before, my heart filled with a silent shame. We drove farther and my mind reflected on the road I'd taken since that time. The journey I chose, the choices I've made, the pain I've caused, and the battle I'm faced with. I knew something had to change.

As the prison bus barreled down the I-15 corridor I began feeling a glimmer of peace within me. We cruised by the southern Utah mountains and finally pulled into the Beaver County Correctional Facility. I was unloaded from the van and walked into this unfamiliar facility.

No familiar faces, no clue what was next, but with the promise I made to my son on my mind I clinched my teeth and held my head up high. I knew what I had to do. I didn't know how I was going to do it but I knew in my heart what needed to be done.

I was booked in and escorted through a maze of hallways. Finally, I walked into the section and made my way to the cell where I'd be resting my neck for a little while. As the days ticked by I discovered that I'd been screened and selected for the inmate placement program, a system where prison inmates are transferred to county jails across the state. Designed to help control the rapidly increasing prison population.

So, there I was, incarcerated in the middle of the Utah desert and desperately trying to hold my life on the outside together. But I knew it was all spun together by a web of lies and it was only a matter of time until I lost it all. I desperately needed help so I put in a request to enter the facilities in-patient drug treatment program. By the fourth of August 2011, I was accepted and entered rehab. I entered with a newfound resolve and commitment to give this all I've got, to learn all I could, and become a better man.

It was a seven-month program with classes eight hours a day. I approached treatment with an openness and humility, which served me well as the days pressed on. I was told things that were hard for me to hear, but they were things I needed to hear, because they helped me grow. My emotions also started to surface. It felt good to feel again, I had almost forgotten what it felt like. It also felt good to start being honest. I was surrounded by men who had lost their way and were spilling their hearts and sharing their pain, in hopes of finding their way back.

At that crucial point in my recovery I was blessed to have a few great men to look up to. I feel blessed because, so often the norm in the prison system is to be surrounded by negativity, cynicism, anger, and violence.

It's a blessing to find someone who chooses to stand tall against the winds of negativity and the depths of despair. There was one man whose example had a big impact on me. His name is Josh. He did the right thing even when he thought no one was watching, his character struck me as a man who'd had enough and wanted something different.

I continually watched him stand up for what he knew in his heart was right. I remember thinking, 'I want to be a man like that, a man my son can be proud of.'

He was a leader in the program by title and by example. Each morning he stood in front of the group and shared experience and direction. He expressed the importance of character, faith, integrity, and courage. I am indebted to this man, and beyond grateful for his example to me during a time when I needed it the most.

While I experienced growth and strength within, my life outside was full of chaos. My son's fourth birthday came and went, and of course, I wasn't there. I broke his heart a little more each day. My marriage was on the rocks, tensely held together in anticipation for the outcome of my hearing with the board of pardons. It was scheduled for the first week of December, and I fearfully awaited that day knowing I was facing up to fifteen years in prison.

My life choices had caught up to me and it was time for me to finally pay the piper. Over the past twelve years my addiction continually grew into a force within me that threatened my very existence, and finally I began to awaken the warrior within me.

I was finally getting help, but I wondered just what the future held. I wondered when the storm surrounding me would run out of rain. I wondered when the waves would stop pounding, and if I would have the faith and the strength to endure to the end. Little did I know; the storm clouds were still only building.

Have I Had Enough?

22

'My Hero'

'What do you want to be remembered for?'

Elden Gabriel Price was born in June of 1927. He entered this world in a time of growth, discovery, and principle. I feel humbled and honored to call this rock of a man, my grandpa and my hero. On Memorial Day 1950, filled with chivalry and class, he proposed to his sweetheart (my grandma). They were married in the following months and began a beautiful legacy.

They had nine children together, my mother was the fourth child. Grandpa put his family first. He let his life speak through his loving example. He and his sweetheart raised their children in a home of faith, tradition, honor, humility, dedication, and, most importantly, love.

He loved to serve and he taught those he loved how to serve. He fiercely loved his family, his God, and his country. Honorably serving in World War II. He also served missions for his faith. He first served in the eastern states. He and his sweetheart also served missions together in the Pacific Northwest, the Philippine Islands, and the church offices in Salt Lake City.

Each day in my grandpa's life was one of service and love. When I was around him I felt like I was the most important person in the world. I know he had that effect on so many. I admire the way he adored his sweetheart. After sixty-one years of marriage there still was never a door he didn't open for her, or a day that went by when he didn't tell her how beautiful she is.

This gentle giant will always be my hero. Of the thirty-two grandchildren and forty-six great-grandchildren there is yet to be one that doesn't have a touching experience of how he was also, their hero.

This kind man is one of the greatest influences of my life. I admire his resounding character. He was honorable, dependable, humble, faithful, loving, diligent, and true. I love him so very much.

As I sit inside the walls of this cell today, and write these words on this page, I can feel his love. As I write this I feel grateful to call him my hero. He is a warrior in my eyes. But as I write the words of this brief passage, detailing a few parts of my grandpa's life, I also see these mere words can only make a futile attempt to sum up the man my grandpa truly is. Nevertheless, he stood as tall as any and humbly walked his path. I love him dearly.

On October 19th 2011, I received a page from the officers telling me I needed to call my wife immediately, it was urgent. Upon hearing those instructions, my heart immediately dropped and my mind thought of the horrific list of possibilities. I scrambled to the phone and called her. She told me that it was my grandpa. He was in the hospital and not doing well. I felt helpless, I felt concern for my mom and for my grandma, and I felt like I was a million miles away.

A few hours later I was blessed with the chance to speak with my hero one last time. Over the phone, I told him I love him and how much he means to me.

He stands so tall in my eyes. I felt his love through the phone that day. He slipped into the eternities a few hours later and as he departed he was surrounded by his family.

His sweetheart held him in her loving arms, he smiled with his last breath for a life well lived, and he passed away in peace.

That night, I laid in my cell, tossing and turning. I got up and stared out the window for a moment, then I would pace my cell, feeling helpless and trapped. I knew I needed to be there for my mom, for my precious grandma, for my sister, for my brothers, and for my family. I wanted to give my grandpa a giant hug, see the love in his kind eyes, and tell him how much I love him. 'What have I done!?...aaahhh!!'

There are times when your family needs you and there are times like this when your family really needs you, and I wasn't there. I was stuck in a cell when they needed me the most, and I needed them. My heart broke for my family.

I had created my own little hell on earth, I wanted to numb the hurt I felt. I wanted to escape the pain.

I could hear the opposing force urging me to give up, whispering, *'Give in, you can find drugs in here, you're not worth it, you're not even there for your family, give up, give in, find some pills, find some chew, something, anything, escape the pain, you need it, you need me.'*

I could feel those thoughts getting more callous and more daring. But for the first time in my life I recognized them for what they were, I knew they were not me. Then, I heard my **'Warrior Within'** finally wake up and say 'No! <u>I want to live, I am done with that old way of life. No more of this</u>, <u>this ends here</u>!'

A few days after grandpa's passing I experienced an uplifting glimpse of hope. It started out as an average day of groups. We were learning about addiction but I felt like I was on auto-pilot. Then my friend Josh stood up to teach a seminar. He, being a man I looked up to, dialed my attention into what he had to teach. It was set up something like this...

He said, "Close your eyes, let your imagination carry you through this... You're walking down a sidewalk covered by the shade of beautiful trees. The sun occasionally breaks through the leaves and shines warmth on your face. Traffic is backed up around the corner as a line of cars slowly inch their way around the bend and try to find a parking space. People are walking along the sidewalk dressed in suits and Sunday dresses. Holding hands they file into the chapel.

A bit of recognition begins to fill your mind as you see many familiar faces. These are your friends, your family, and your loved ones. Flowers and pictures line the walkway and there is a feeling of love and admiration in the air. As the crowds walk by, you reach for their hand to say hi and you realize they can't see you. Tears are falling down their faces as they comfort each other. You want so badly to hug them and tell them it's okay. You follow them into the chapel and take a seat towards the back. As you take in the scene, you come to the stunning realization that you are at a funeral, and it is your own. You see pictures from your life, your birth, and along your journey to the end.

Memories flash in your mind of the journey of your life. Then your loved ones stand and express their thoughts of you and the life you chose to live. What is said? What are you remembered for? What kind of person were you along your brief journey here on earth?'

And as I sat there in the still darkness, listening to this meditation, I thought of my grandpa and the life he lived. His funeral was happening soon and I thought of how my family must be feeling. I felt my eyes start raining tears, and I just let them flow. I thought of all the times I came so close to death. The tears fell harder and harder. It felt good to just let them fall, so I sat there in silence and let the tears keep falling. Without holding back and without wiping them off my face, the tears fell, and fell, and fell.

We were then instructed to write down what we would want said about us at our funeral. Given the profound prompt of, 'What do you want to be remembered for?'

As I began to write I felt the comfort of my hero. His life spoke to me and inspired me as the ink flowed on the paper. I truly felt his love.

I wrote about the man I knew in my heart I was capable of being. I wrote about the man I was designed to be. I wrote things that are dear to my heart to this day. I thought, 'If I were to die today, what would be said about me? How would that differ from the eulogy I just wrote?'

I'm grateful for that meeting. It couldn't have come at a more perfect time in my life. A time where I was utterly broken.

I looked at myself in the mirror that night and the face looking back at me looked beaten and worn, but in my eyes, I saw the spark of light, a light I'd thought was gone for good.

It was the fire of life, the fire of purpose, the fire to stand up and be counted. I could feel the Warrior Within awakening.

Have I Had Enough?

23

'Learning to Stand Tall'

"Stand for something or you'll fall for anything."

As the days turned into weeks, I was faced with different battles regularly. One thing I was beginning to learn was that I felt good when I chose to stand tall and do what I knew in my heart was right. I was learning, growing, and beginning to experience the light of hope and strength.

A few weeks later my friend and mentor, Josh, graduated from the program. It was hard to see him go because he stood so tall in my eyes, but I am so grateful for his example.

Before leaving, he and the program coordinator pulled me to the side and asked me if I would be willing to step up and take his place as a leader for the program. I felt a bit nervous, but I was excited for the opportunity to grow, so I accepted the challenge. I had some big shoes to fill but knew in my heart that It would be a great opportunity to lead, to learn, to serve, and to grow. These were all things I so desperately needed at that critical point in my recovery.

As a leader, I was faced with many new challenges. These challenges were uncomfortable at times, but the vulnerability I felt was challenging me to grow. Facing challenges sober was something I had never done.

Every morning before our group I stood and shared thoughts and goals for the day. At night, I got lost in researching, studying, and preparing my thoughts for the next day. Fascination came over me as I immersed in the wisdom of the ancients. So much has been passed down from the ancients, urging us to awaken our capacities

I experienced clarity, focus, and peace as I read, studied, and applied it to my life. I began discovering, for myself, that when we truly believe with all our hearts in what we're saying, the words we speak are heard, felt, and accepted. I reached a point in my life where I was finally willing to try anything and everything to change my life, so I dove in.

The treatment program I was in was a humbling environment. Each of us had made it here to prison, each on our own separate journey, but all somehow so similarly connected. We were all in the fight of our lives, addiction.

During the days, as we held classes and shared experiences with each other, there were a wide range of emotions felt. A deep and raw emotion that can only be found in the rooms of recovery. The hope was tangible. We shed tears together, thinking of the ones we love and the hurt we've caused them. I felt a strengthening bond with the others in there.

For the first time in my life I began to learn about addiction. My counselor, Don Lankford, shared his research and insight into addiction with me, it really opened my eyes to the beast of addiction. Helping me understand why this disease was in my mind, and what it was. They say you must know your enemy. It felt good to learn about what I'd been fighting my whole life.

I felt peace knowing that I was doing what I knew in my heart was right.

I knew I wanted to make a difference and I felt tired of the old me, it was time to start being the man I was designed to be.

As the weeks pressed on I felt the clouds of my addiction begin to disperse. I was finally getting to know my true self again. It felt so good to be me, the authentic me.

But my life outside the walls was crumbling. I could feel the distance between my wife and I, growing further by the day. I knew I had caused her entirely too much heartache and pain. But within me, inside my mind, my heart, and my soul I could feel a change taking place, in the depths of my being. And with that feeling I began to experience peace. I felt grace, I felt hope, I felt love, and I felt the will to take another step, and then another.

As the end of November 2011 approached I felt nervous for my upcoming hearing with the Board of Pardons. It was only a few days away and I knew the outcome would decide just how long I would be locked away. With that on my mind, I prepared a thought for the next morning.

Late that night, as I studied and read, I came across a quote that caused me to think very deeply, so I prepared to read it the next morning. When that morning came, I stood in front of the group and read,

"You can map out a fight plan or a life plan, but when the action starts it may not go the way you planned and you're down to your reflexes_ which means your training, that's where your road work shows. If you cheated on that in the dark of the morning, well, you're getting found out now, beneath the bright lights."

-Joe Frazier

We discussed how this, right now, is the dark of the morning and how nobody really knows what we're doing or the true thoughts and intents of our hearts.

Whether we choose to cheat this experience, or stand tall through it, those brilliant lights will still inevitably shine. I related to them how bright those lights can be. I told the guys of my experience as my face was plastered across the ten-o'clock news, and how degraded I felt as I was found out *beneath the bright lights.*

We also talked of hope and vision, for when those bright lights shine and we can hold our heads high, standing tall, knowing that we did our best, that we did what we knew in our hearts was right, and changed our lives. Those bright lights can motivate and inspire us to give this all we've got, today, in this *dark of the morning.*

That evening the snow gently fell across the valley. I stood by the window in my cell, watching the sun set to the west over the snow-covered fields and mountains of southern Utah. Although I watched this, through chain-link and barb-wire, the scene gave me hope. Tomorrow was a big day, my day of reckoning.

That night I tossed and turned, thinking of the journey that led me here. My thoughts were lost in all the possibilities my future held. Then, as I found myself staring at the concrete and cinderblock, I began to pray for comfort and peace. As I prayed I felt a calmness in my heart, my eyelids eventually getting heavy, and I drifted off to sleep.

Have I Had Enough?

24

'Day of Reckoning'

"No matter how much you change you still gotta pay the price for the things you've done. So, it looks like I've got a long road ahead, but I'll be seein ya; this side or the other."

-Ben Affleck (<u>the town</u>)

I woke-up that next morning with an anxious feeling in my gut. I was nervous for the hearing that would decide what my prison sentence would be. So, I put one foot in front of the other and got prepared for the day.

During the morning meeting, I stood up and shared my feelings for the day. As I stood up there I felt exposed and vulnerable, but had the strength to lay my heart out on the table.

For reasons I don't quite know, I decided to share my story. My eyes pooled with tears felt as I thought back to that cold morning on the side of the interstate. In that moment, I could almost feel the rain washing over my lifeless body.

I talked about the battle I fight within and of those deceitful whispers from the opposing force. I spoke about the weight of the lies I told, and the fear I felt each day I was on the run. I can still so vividly remember the suffocating fear I felt each time I looked in the rearview mirror. Running from the future and trying to escape the past.

With the weight of those thoughts on my mind, I expressed the pain I feel, knowing my sos heart is breaking more and more every day I'm gone.

I stood in front of those men that morning feeling a wave of emotion crash upon me and remember thinking, 'When is enough, enough?' Within the depths of my core, I was blessed with peace. In that moment, I knew what I needed to do.

My stomach seized up in knots when a few moments later I was told to head down to my parole hearing. Time seemed to slow as I began to walk down the hallway. I remember my ears felt deaf to all sound except for the beat of my heart, pounding so fast. I thought, 'This is it.'

I was shackled and placed in a small holding cell with four other men. I tried thinking of some staged rehearsal of what to say, but my mind just went blank. One by one, the others were called out and escorted to their hearing, until finally, I was the last one left. I was alone in the cell with my thoughts, my fears, and my hopes. In that moment, I prayed. I prayed with all my heart. I prayed not for an early release, not for what I thought was best, but for what I needed to change my life. I felt so tired of fighting, so tired of hurting, and I knew it was time to finally surrender to God's will.

In that moment, I felt a calming peace enter my heart unlike anything I've ever felt before. I sat there shackled on the cold concrete feeling a warm embrace of comfort.

I believe what I felt was the presence of my hero; my grandpa Elden Price. I felt his warm hands on my shoulders bringing peace and strength to every fiber of my being. Then I felt a clear and calm thought enter my mind saying, 'Endure this well, everything is going to be okay.'

I felt the support of all the universe urging me to stand tall. That experience is personal to me, and one I'll cherish in my heart forever.

Finally, my time was up and I was escorted into the court room. As I entered the room I saw my sister, my mom, and then my dad. Man, I've put them through hell.

I sat down in the chair and looked up to my hearing officer. I felt peace in my heart and heard the resounding prompting to be brutally honest. He asked me about my life, my crimes, and about my addiction. I sat there in that chair and thought about the path I've walked. Then, after all these years, after all the lies, and after all the secrets; I finally came clean.

I'd been lying to everyone for far too long. I hid my addiction, I lied about my involvement in the robbery, and no one knew just how out-of-control I'd become. I thought I had everyone fooled, but the only fool was me. But those lies were done now, I finally came clean and told the truth. As soon as I spoke the truth I felt the weight of the world lifting from my shoulders.

The hearing officer said that, even though it was encouraging that I made some changes, the crimes I committed were very serious. He recommended I serve a prison sentence of about four-and-a-half years.

I walked toward the exit of that court room feeling full of emotions but I held my head high. I felt freedom even though I was shackled and imprisoned. I felt comfort and faith in knowing that I'll be released the day I'm ready, though it looks like I've got a long road ahead.

Just before exiting the court room I looked back and saw my family with tears in their eyes. I can only imagine the feeling they felt as they watched me finally face my past. As I walked past them I could see heartbreak in their eyes. So many emotions flooded over me as I walked out of that room, then I distinctly remember feeling a wave of peace.

I was granted a visit immediately following the hearing. I entered the visit and for a while we just looked at each other through the window pane.

I felt for my sister as her eyes were covered in tears. I've put her through so much. Then I looked to my Mom, her eyes showed wisdom and love. I could see she wanted with all her loving heart for this nightmare to end. I felt from her eyes that she could see the good in me that no one else, including me, could see. Then, I saw my Dad, with his love and his strength, wanting with all he had to shoulder the pain for me. We all cried, and healed in that moment.

That was the first time my mom and dad were standing side-by-side in such a sensitive situation, since the divorce when I was twelve. The tragedy of my choices brought them here to this jail, and to this heartbreaking moment.

I looked them in the eyes and saw pain and worry, but I could feel hope. I felt a calming comfort amidst the heartache. The feelings of peace I felt within echoed my decision. I was making good on the promise I made to my son, and only my conscience knows how true to that decision I am.

During the visit, I could see my dad was very emotional. Even with all his strength I could see his heart was breaking as he yearned to carry my burdens. He said, 'I am so sorry son. Since your mother and I divorced...' and, mid-sentence, I had a stunning realization that I'd been using my parents' divorce as a crutch to blame all my problems. It was time to throw that crutch away and stand on my own two feet.

So, I cut my dad off and said, 'No more. I made the choices that got me here, I knew the consequences, and I still chose to do it. I was taught right from wrong. This isn't your fault, this isn't mom's fault, I made the choices that got me here and I'm making the choice that will get me out of here. I'm done using that as my excuse.'

The liberation I felt after finally taking responsibility was something I'll never forget.

The four of us shared tears in the visit and we shared strength. I think it was good for them to see I'd embraced the challenge. The visit ended and we said our goodbyes, but before walking out I expressed with conviction that, no matter what, my life may crumble out there, but one thing I know is certain; I'm giving this everything I've got and I'm coming out of here a better man.

I left the visit feeling renewed and recharged. As I walked down the halls I felt lighter on my feet. I knew I was up against the biggest challenge of my life, knowing I would receive confirmation of my parole date soon, and deep down I knew what the outcome would be, I had my fingers crossed but thought...

I'll be released the day I'm ready, so it's time to get busy.

Have I Had Enough?

25

'Let It Burn'

"The question for each man to settle is not what he would do if he had means, time, influence, and educational advantages. The question is what he will do with the things he has. The moment a young man ceases to dream or bemoan his lack of opportunities, and resolutely looks his conditions in the face and resolves to change them, he lays the cornerstone of a solid and honorable success."

-Hamilton Wright Mabie

My confirmation from the Board of Pardons came that following week. The first words from my caseworker were, 'Ryan you are not going to like this.' So, I sat down on a chair and braced for the news. I read my confirmation paper and it stated that I was granted parole on September eighth, 2015. That was almost four more years away.

I felt overwhelmed as I tried to let the news sink in. I completely failed the attempt to wrap my mind around the time, all I could think about was my son. My heart broke for him. He was three years old when I left to prison, and with this date, I would be released just days after his eighth birthday.

I felt numb. During the next few days I was overcome by an unmatched vulnerability. It wasn't a loneliness, per-se, it was a new understanding that it was up to me, and it was my time to step up. Maybe it was that I wasn't in the habit of taking responsibility, and, by finally taking responsibility, I felt alone? I don't know, but it was an exhausting time for me.

I heard the whispers of the opposing force, *'give up, it's not worth it, you're not worth it, nobody cares, it doesn't matter, you don't matter, you need it, you need me.'*

There was a part of me that wanted to listen to those whispers, for it was what I knew best. But the Warrior Within me told me, 'I've come too far. I'm not giving up. I am worth it. I can, and I will breakthrough!'

I sat alone in my cell and began writing what I was feeling. The pages in my journal began to fill with ink and emotion. In the distance, I heard Christmas songs echoing from the television. I missed home so much, I missed my family. I looked over to the little metal desk and saw a letter I had written in group. This letter was like the one I'd written years earlier, from the perspective of my son and what he must be going through.

It amazes me how quickly the past repeats itself if we don't change. I picked it up, held it in my hand, and began to read while my heart filled with tears. It read,

'Daddy,

Mom said you might be home for Christmas. When are you coming home daddy? I miss going on drives with you, listening to songs, and going to Boondocks with you on the weekends driving race cars.

I want you back dad.

I love chasing you around in the house in my Batman PJ's. I got new PJs because I got bigger. See, look dad I'm bigger now! I can do all the things that I always wanted to. But most of all I miss you dad and I'm sad that you're gone and I wish and pray for you to come home.

Why did you leave? Do you still love me? If so, why are you not here with me..?

Anyways, I sure love you dad. I'm going to go play now. Bye.

Love,
Dominic

I sat there in my cell and let the tears fall.

"What lies behind us, and what lies before us, are tiny matters compared to what lies within us."
                                                              -Oliver Holmes

About a week-and-a-half later, I decided to finally call home. It was the final straw when I broke the crushing news to my wife. Everything came crumbling down. I completely shattered her heart with the news.

The guilt I felt at that time cut very deep, the wounds were still so fresh.

I sat in my cell as my mind played tapes of what my family must be going through. I cried, I got angry, I got sad, and I got frustrated. Inside I began to feel like I was losing it.

That night, when the sun began to set majestically in the west, over the snow-covered fields and mountains of southern Utah, I began to feel a moment of peace.

Although I watched it through the barbwire and chain-link, I was blessed to feel a glimmer of hope. In that moment, I prayed, with all the faith I could muster and from a place deep down within me, I surrendered.

I looked out the window and said, 'I am grateful for this opportunity I've been blessed with to change my life. Help me God, I've had enough.' In that moment, I knew in my heart that I was not alone.

During the following weeks, all I could manage to do was put one foot in front of the other. The water around me seemed deeper than ever and the mountain before me seemed bigger than I'd ever seen. So, I began to turn my feet in the right direction, put my trust in God, and take a step. One step at a time, trusting and surrendering to His will.

On Christmas I received an envelope with two letters inside. One was from my son, and the other was from my wife. I opened them from my cell and for a while I just stared blankly at them. I was in no hurry to open them and could feel a deep foreboding. But finally, I succumbed to the anticipation, and opened the letter from my son. My heart melted as I read his loving words. He wished me a merry Christmas and he included some drawings and a picture of him on Santa's lap.

After reading it I tried to imagine how difficult it must have been for my heartbroken wife to help him write how much he missed me.

For a long while I could only stare at the other un-opened letter. I finally opened it and began to read.

In the letter, my wife expressed the pain she felt and that she just couldn't take it anymore. She said she's moving on, our goals, our dreams, and our vision boards, gone, thrown away, because they were all lies.

I sat there in my cell and finally began to glimpse the reality of just how much I hurt her. At one time, she was my queen, and now, I shattered her heart beyond repair.

The pain I felt that Christmas week opened my heart to a pathway of an entire change of life. It's as if, amidst all the pain, my heart surrendered and was touched by the infinite love of my God. I knew, from that moment, that what I had to do was strengthen my faith, and trust in His will.

That week, as I watched the snow continue to fall across the fields, my mind, heart, and spirit reflected and prayed. I thought, 'How do I make this count? I'm ready, what do I need to do?' And as I contemplated my plans I could feel the pain motivating me to action. The pain I was feeling was serving as a catalyst to fuel my journey.

That first week of the new year I got a message from an officer to call my wife. As I approached the phone I felt apprehensive, but as I dialed the number and it rang, my heart dropped. I had a feeling what this was about, part of me wanted to just hang up, but no, I'd been running for far too long. Bianca picked up and said, 'I wanted to call you and tell you, divorce papers are in the mail, I wanted you to hear it first from me.'

Even during this horrible situation, she chose to handle it with grace, dignity, and class. I am so grateful for her. We cried together once she was finished, and then we proceeded to have one of the most healthy, open, honest, and understanding conversations we've ever had. We made commitments to each other, to be kind, to not make this a mean divorce, and to do our best to not bad-mouth each other. Thinking of our son we made commitments to do what was best for him.

That call was devastating but part of me still felt peace within. It must have been such a tough call for her to make. She was now a single mother, carrying a heavy burden on her shoulders. The papers arrived on the tenth of January. When I held the papers in my hand I could feel the finality. The divorce was tangible and it hurt, the pain stinging deeply within.

Again, it was time for me to find a way to trust His will.

Have I Had Enough?

26

'Be Tall, Be Strong, Be True'

"You can give up that one thing and you'll have everything; or you can have that one thing but you'll lose everything."
-unknown

Two days later I experienced what I believe was Divine providence working in my life. I was getting close to graduation from the treatment program and would then be faced with the decision of where to go and what to do next during my prison term.

I was called down to a meeting with the four program coordinators. They expressed their belief in me, and agreed that I would be a good candidate to fill the shoes of the coordinator that was paroling. He had served nearly three years as coordinator.

I knew it would be a huge responsibility and I knew it would challenge me in so many ways, but within me I felt excited and up to the challenge. So, I accepted the offer knowing in my heart that it was an answer to so many prayers.

Without fail, I heard the whispers of the opposing force urging me to give up, to give in, and to cheat this experience. But the warrior within me began to trump those negative thoughts. I knew this opportunity would help me learn, grow, and stand tall. If I could just do the things I knew in my heart were right.

Standing tall, doing what's right, being authentic? What do these truly mean? These questions filled my mind, and for me, it meant doing the uncomfortable thing, and sometimes the unpopular thing.

I received a letter from my sister a few days later, tucked inside the letter was a copy of something she had discovered while going through her things at home. It was a family creed our mom wrote for us back in 1996, placing it on our living room wall, so many years before.

Long forgotten from the recesses of my conscious mind, its truth lay somewhere deep within, waiting to be awakened.

It read...

'**Be tall**.

Because you are, stand above in humility and grace, powerfully be proud of who you are and what you represent.

Be strong.

Take care of your body because it's your only one, let the warrior within come out and be present in word, action, and thought.

Be true.

To your word, your actions, and your belief. Always be honest in who you believe you are.

Be tall, Be strong, Be true.'

-Ruth Price 1996 (mom)

I am grateful for those empowering words, planted in my heart so many years earlier. My sister sent the letter at the perfect time in my life.

I knew this next four years would be tough, but I also knew it could be used as an opportunity, to lay the foundation of a successful life. Some days I felt like I just couldn't go on anymore, other days were filled with hope and renewed strength. Through the peaks and valleys of each day I began to feel stronger each time I stayed the course and held on with faith.

Though my body was imprisoned, my mind, heart, and spirit felt free. The time I spent in treatment was productive and healthy for me. I was learning how to stand for what I believe in. My habits were being refined, my faith was being strengthened, and I began to feel Gods loving hand in my life. It's clear to see that I was being watched over and carried along my path.

I began experiencing a powerful strength in the rooms of recovery. We grew together as a group, a few guys just trying to find a better way I guess. We all had our own unique story but in a way it was all so similar. Most of us had 'spilt the same blood in the same mud' as the saying goes, but now our hearts were screaming for change.

As I would speak out about change, I remember feeling so many deep emotions rising to the surface. Oftentimes I would take a moment and picture my son, looking on at me, watching how I was being. I'd think, 'Am I being the type of man I'd want my son to be?

I was blessed in my journey to come across a very good man, named Cy. I look up to him and am grateful for his insight and friendship. He had a question he consciously thought throughout the day, he'd ask, 'Am I acting in the way my kids would be proud of?' What an empowering question! That simple question helped him to stay grounded with his values. I am so grateful for the example he is to me.

Meanwhile, the days were turning into weeks, and the weeks were turning into months, and I was getting stronger. It felt so good to finally be doing what I believed in my heart was right.

As I strengthened those habits of doing what I knew was right, it became easier the next time. But I had wanted to change before, only to fall back. What was different this time?

I had a long time ahead of me, in the prison system, so I wondered, 'Would I choose to stand firm? Would I choose to strengthen or would I choose to give up? Would I choose to go forward or would I choose to go back?

Have I Had Enough?

27

'I've Had Enough'

"Addicts persist in their self-destructive, addictive behaviors, until something within themselves, something quite apart from anyone else's efforts, changes so radically that the desire for the high is dulled and ultimately deadened by the desire for a better life."
-Beverly Conyers

Over the course of the following year I found myself being continually challenged. With each new challenge, I experienced growth and strength as I stayed the course.

In January of 2013, I was asked by some of the officers at the jail if I would to speak at two of their surrounding high-schools. I was asked to share my thoughts on addiction and its role in bringing me to prison. I felt nervous but quickly agreed. It was time to share my story.

As we drove away from the Jail my heart began to race. I said a silent prayer in my heart for comfort and the ability to say something that would help these young men and women at their assembly.

I felt impressed to share a few moments of my story, openly with them, as I remembered how I felt when I was their age. Every seat in the assembly hall was silent, all you could hear was the sound of my heartbeat through the microphone, and my laboring breath. I held the microphone so tight.

I stood there in my prison whites, feeling humbled and vulnerable, carrying the look of a man worn from battle. I was flanked to my left by police officers and faculty. Everyone was silently anticipating my answer to the young man's question, 'Have I Had Enough?'

Flash backs and scenes from my life flashed vividly in my mind. I'm sure you could see the pain I felt written across the darkness in my eyes; reflecting the battle I fought within. Standing alone on stage, I pictured my son sitting in the crowd. I remembered the promise I'd made to him the last time I held him in my arms.

'I'm going to do everything I can to make this count.'

Alone on the stage my heart pounded, partly from the nerves and partly from the passion I felt for what I was saying. My stomach was tense, feeling more vulnerable than I've ever felt before, but a part of me took it head-on and stood firm. I could feel a deep-rooted peace and resolve burning within me as I proceeded to answer the young man's question.

"You'd think, after lying there in the rain on the side of the interstate that cold lonely morning so long ago, that I would have had enough. Or you'd think, after being strapped to gurney, after gurney, ambulance ride after ambulance ride, that I would have had enough. But no, I kept going back.

Or you'd think after breaking the precious hearts of all those who love me, again, and again, and again, that I couldn't possibly have thoughts to use. But no, I kept going back. The shit just kept getting deeper and the lies just kept getting bigger. Most people would have had enough, but not me, I kept going back. I kept breaking the hearts of all those around me.

Countless sleepless nights they rested their heads on tear soaked pillows, praying for me to change, but I was barely scratching the surface of the pain I've caused.

It gets deeper. Imagine a mom, with so much love, searching, seeking, hoping, and waiting for her son to wake up and discover his true purpose and place in this world.

Or imagine a dad, on his knees day and night, with a heart full of faith and hope, just waiting for his son to step up. Hoping it's not too late. Layer after layer, heart after heart, the hurt always cuts deeper.

When is enough enough?

Or, you'd think, after I careened my car through a telephone-pole, at sixty miles-per-hour, carnage and destruction all around me, that I surely must have had enough, right?

Or the years after years I wasted in jail or on the run, overdose after overdose. The lies I told, the tears my family cried, heartbreak after piercing heartbreak. Until those around me became calloused from the pain and then, here I'd come again, like a wrecking ball...WHAAMMM!! I'd shatter their hearts again. I created a world of pain, but I still hadn't had enough..."

I paused my reply as I felt such an intense wave of emotion come over me. I felt tears welling in my eyes but managed to hold my composure, best I could, and continued.

"The moment for me came as I watched my beautiful little boy, my son, my little super-hero, run and play in the backyard. He laughed and smiled so bright. I stood there on the corner watching him as I was dying on the inside. I prepared to say goodbye, knowing I was going to crush his little heart. As I held my son in my arms that day and tried to say goodbye, he looked me in the eyes and he ended up holding me that day. I was broken. The pain I felt is so real and it finally stung deep enough. It reached into a place deep within me that knew I needed to change.

I don't claim to have it worse than the next guy and I don't claim that it can't get any worse than where it's at either, in fact, I'm far from it

I'm a regular guy who made some horrible choices and, for me, what I went through was hell on earth. The pain I felt seared the depths of my soul, finally reaching a part of me that decided that I just couldn't take it anymore. The pain finally stung deep enough.

For me,

I've Had Enough.

Part III

'Strengthening

the

Warrior Within'

28

'So, Now What?'

What do we do when we say we've had enough? I think about that question often, as the days pass in here. One thing I do know is that any one person's addiction or their own internal battle, is uniquely complex and personal. No one person's story is the same, and no one person's battle is the same.

I believe in recovery. With every fiber of my being, I believe it is possible. The destination is a continual, life-long journey.

Through the years in here, I've experienced moments of pure hope, strength, and a calming peace within. I've also experienced moments of doubt, discouragement, and utter despair.

With this constant ebb n' flow, the highs and lows of life, and just the overall pressures of life I wonder, 'How can I stay the course? How can I make this count? How can I tap into my hidden capacity and be the man I'm designed to be?'

As I contemplate these thoughts, I also realize that the storms of life still come. We are all faced with trials along our journey, just because we've *had enough,* doesn't mean it's all sunshine from there on out, in fact, far from it. For me, at times it feels like, since I've had enough, and have been making changes, the opposing force has been pulling out all the stops. Continuously trying to lure me off the path I've chosen.

So, how can we stay the course? How can we stand tall amidst life's challenges? How can we live a life free from the clutches of addiction?

Since you're reading this book you know of the pain in addiction. Either from my personal story, or maybe you struggle with addiction, or maybe someone very close to you is stuck in the clutches of addiction. It rips apart communities, it rips apart families, and it rips one's heart and soul to pieces. So much so, that I felt impassioned to write my story in hopes that something in it has touched your heart and in some way brought hope to your journey.

We are all unique in our own personal way. I believe we are all, of infinite worth. I also believe that along life's path it is up to us, individually to seek and discover truth of our own volition.

Things click differently for each of us, especially when dealing with something as complex and personal as addiction. I believe it's imperative to be open and to discover that truth <u>for ourselves</u>.

Throughout the complexities of my addiction I'm finding, for me, it's best if I keep it simple.

Part three of this book discusses some of my experiences with a few simple concepts that are helping me awaken to a place where I can believe in myself. Helping me nurture that precious internal harmony between my conscience and my-self. With these I'm beginning to discover a place of peace wherein lies the faith to surrender my will, and put my trust in my God.

From a conceptual standpoint, this wisdom has been passed down from the ancients. I'm grateful for those who have come before, their wisdom and faith inspires me. These concepts, practices, and thoughts are helping me along my path each day, and help me stay the course.

My hope and prayer is that you can experience strength and hope along your journey as you discover <u>your</u> truth, discover <u>your</u> passion, and discover <u>your</u> purpose.

May you enjoy the final pages of this book. My humble prayer is that something in this book has helped you in your journey to answer some of life's toughest questions. May <u>you</u> seek, search, and find <u>your</u> truth.

"Watch your thoughts, they become Words.

Watch your words, they become Actions.

Watch your actions, they become Habits.

Watch your habits, they become Character.

Watch your character, it becomes your Destiny."

-Lao Tzu

29

'Watch your Thoughts'

"We cannot perform outwardly in a way that is inconsistent with how we think inwardly. You cannot be what you believe you aren't. But, here's the good news: you can change your thinking and as a result, your life."

-John C. Maxwell

As I reflect upon my life, I'm able to glimpse how impactful my thoughts have been. In fact, as I trace back the to the decisions I made that landed me in jails, hospitals, or one of a hundred other horrible situations, I find those decisions all began with a thought.

The mind is a beautiful thing, a miracle in every sense of the word, a beautiful gift; but it can also be a devastating curse, if we don't nurture it and use it wisely.

Something I'm learning is the fact that thoughts are things. What we think, in turn, creates our reality. As I journey through my recovery I am constantly reminded to guard my thoughts or to *master* my thoughts, for me that's where it all begins.

Every moment we fill our mind with an ongoing stream of thought. The dominant thoughts then reproduce themselves into actions, which in turn create our reality. So, how can we bypass the brains tendency to focus on the negative? Especially when those enticing whispers of addiction tell us we are not enough?

When we plant a thought, we reap an act. How can we consciously plant thoughts that will empower us, strengthen us, and help us to live the life we ultimately desire?

Think of what an amazing gift the human mind is, right now, as you read this book, you're thinking. Your mind is processing what you read, and as you think you also have the power to direct those thoughts, in-turn, creating your reality. And the reality is, as I write these words on this page I sit behind concrete walls and chain link fence. I'm away from all those I love, a product of my thoughts. But even as I sit here, I can decide now, that I am ready to live a life of happiness and congruency within. With my thoughts, today, I am creating a better reality for my future. Since it all begins in the mind, how can we consciously nurture the garden of our minds?

Perspective

No matter where you are right now, no matter what you're doing, who you are, or how much pain you feel, no matter how hopeless you may feel, no matter what your circumstance may be, you have, installed within you, the gift and ability to frame your experiences. The knowledge of that fact can help us tremendously in our recovery.

> *"If you change the way you look at thing, the things you look at change."*

> -Wayne Dyer

I believe the way we choose to frame life's circumstances will help determine the outcome. This is especially important when we find ourselves in challenging or difficult circumstances.

How we choose to view the journey will manifest itself in the steps we take, and what we can gain from it. If we choose to look at it as hopeless, negative, and full of despair; we're probably right. But on the other hand, if we choose to embrace the journey as something positive, necessary, worthwhile, hopeful, or a gift; then guess what, we're probably right.

Now this isn't meant to be a hokie magic trick saying that all things are perfect just because we choose to think positive. In fact, far from it. Trials still appear and we will be continually faced with challenges. Such is the nature of life. But there is *magic* in it.

I'm experiencing some of that *magic* now. During these years in prison I've adopted a practice that helps me stay grounded.

I practice this typically when the sun is setting in the west, but it could be at any time of day. I look out the window, past the concrete and chain-link, breath consciously, and focus my thoughts. Then, I repeat in my mind, and in my heart, with all the passion, faith, and feeling I can muster,

"I am grateful for this opportunity I have been blessed with, to change my life."

That prayer of gratitude helps me frame this experience differently. As opposed to becoming bitter, hardened, and resentful, it's helping me use this circumstance as an opportunity to change my life.

During those moments of prayer, I feel close to God, I feel love, and I feel hope for a brighter day ahead. Even on the darkest nights, when I feel seeds of fear creeping into my mind, I can shift that thought pattern to one faith.

I challenge you to look deeply into the force of gratitude and prayer. You won't be disappointed. It will completely change how you view your world.

"Gratitude unlocks the fullness of life. It turns what we have into enough and more. It turns denial into acceptance, chaos into order, and confusion into clarity. Gratitude makes sense of our past, brings peace for today, and creates vision for tomorrow."

-Melody Beattie

Purpose

A few years ago, I was given a birthday gift from my mother. Wrapped in a Tuscan box, neatly placed inside was a solid rectangular chunk of polished steel. Engraved along the front it reads...

"What would you attempt to do if you knew you could not fail?"

-Robert H. Schuller

Those words are having a profound effect on my thoughts lately. Years ago, that gift sat on the corner of my desk, and now it's tucked away in a box, with the rest of my things, awaiting my release from prison.

I understand what it feels like to be scattered, or being spread too thin. I understand what it feels like to be thrown about by the winds and waves of life. I've felt the weight of living a lie and knowing deep down that there was another calling for me in life. I've lived a life with no purpose or direction, and it is a tough way to live.

If you've felt that way before, I understand. I've been there too, and it sucks. I believe there are many societal pressures, rooted in fear, that can dim our light and herd us towards conformity. Being aware that there is more to life than just paying bills and dying, my mind is searching and seeking for purpose and meaning in life.

What sparks your soul? What are you curious about? What do you love to do? What do you enjoy? What does the world need? How can you be paid for it?

Behind these prison walls I found my purpose in life. As I've discovered my purpose it's helping me channel my thoughts and focus my energy in ways I never thought possible.

By finding my purpose and putting my soul into it, the distractions of idle thoughts are quickly being replaced by productive and purposeful ones. It's truly a beautiful thing. The compulsion I previously experienced to fill the void I felt with drugs, alcohol, or negativity is now being swallowed up by the passion of my purpose.

Even in this very moment, I'm experiencing the words of my book being written on this page. I believe this book is part of my purpose, but I didn't always believe I could write it. I didn't always believe in myself. But now, as I write these words, I feel an all-encompassing passion whizzing through me like a freight train. Even just the conscious decision to seek and find your purpose, and daily focus on it the discovery, will literally change your life.

"Until a man selects his definite purpose in life he scatters his energy and thoughts. This leads not to power but to indecision and weakness."

-Napoleon Hill

The passion I feel from my purpose is intimately fulfilling. I can feel my thoughts being honed and sharpened to a magnified light. I owe a huge debt of gratitude to Napoleon Hill, and his research into the value of discovering ones' purpose in life. The deep wisdom found in the pages of his books are helping me in more ways than I can mention.

I challenge you to find your purpose, if you haven't already. Make it a priority. They say the first step to getting what you want out of life is to decide what you want. So, decide.

"I know of no more encouraging fact than of man's ability to elevate his life by conscious endeavor."

-Henry David Thoreau

Know yourself. Learn about and discover what you want to do. Then seek, search, and find your purpose. If It is built upon truth, it will last. Ask yourself what you value in life, then build your purpose around those values. See it, visualize it, imagine how it feels to be fulfilled in it, and **believe you can.**

As you discover your purpose, I can testify that the idle thoughts of the mind will begin to dissipate. The enticing whispers of addiction will become easier to stop listening to, because they don't serve you. When the mind and heart are focused on purpose, the negativity and defeatist thoughts begin to simmer down. Energy and passion are channeled to the purpose, enabling the mind and heart to focus on the objective.

As you become anxiously engaged in a life of purpose, the distracting snares of the opposing force will become dulled. The mind becomes free to process and create its purposes as your God will gracefully supply you with the aid you need.

"You have no idea what you're capable of until you try."

-Unknown

You will encounter others along your path that express their doubts in you. It may even be those closest to you. It can feel difficult to stay true to your course but I can guarantee you it is worth it. You have a purpose. It is up to you to discover it, to put your heart into it, and to accomplish it.

"Whatever you do, you need courage. Whatever course you decide upon there is always someone to tell you that you are wrong, there are always difficulties arising that tempt you to believe that your critics are right."

-Ralph Waldo Emerson.

As you come across the various forms of negativity and doubt, remember that God, the universe, and everything in it, are behind you. Smile and wave at the doubters and haters. Remember, <u>you can</u> achieve your purpose and <u>you are</u> destined to leave your mark.

Believe in yourself, believe in your purpose, and build upon it each day with truth and integrity. It's going to take heart, it's going to take courage, and it's going to take the commitment to see it through, but you can do it.

So, what matters most to you? What would you attempt to do if you knew you could not fail? What do you want to be remembered for?

Let your curiosity and imagination lead you. You'll know when you've found it, remember to enjoy the ride of life as you search.

Harnessing the Power of Word

"If we want to change our lives, we have to change the way we think of ourselves. If we want to change the way we think of ourselves, we need to change the way we talk to ourselves."

-*John C. Maxwell*

Our spoken word is an expression of ourselves, the words we suggest to others can and will have a tremendous effect on them, as well as ourselves. I think it is important to always remember that. But how are we treating ourselves? What kind of words are we telling ourselves every minute of every day?

Fresh in my mind are the footprints of the whispers of my addiction. I was lost in the clutches of it, and remember beating myself up mentally, every day. In my mind, I was always telling myself I couldn't do things, that I wasn't worth it, and that I wasn't enough. Before long, the tides of my life were pulled by the current of my negative thoughts, carrying me far away from the life I wanted. My dark thoughts created a dark reality for me, eventually landing myself in a dark prison cell.

So, here I sit, a prisoner of the state, thinking, 'How can I get back on track? How can I train my brain to think better thoughts of myself?' To be honest, I am really challenged with this, but learning to *believe* it more and more as I consciously work on it.

Some incredible things are happening in my life as I consciously retrain my brain. For the first time in my life, I'm experiencing the miracle of believing in myself. I'm finding it easier to stand for my values, achieve my purpose, and to experience true peace within.

I believe it all starts in our thoughts and hearts. It is anchored by a faithful vision of values, dreams, and of purpose. The storms of life will inevitably come and go, but it's during those storms where we fall back on our reinforcements. Something that helps me reinforce my thoughts, values, and vision is my, *"I am..." statement.*

I wrote my "I am..." statement from the context of already being the person I believe I am destined to be. For so long I procrastinated putting it down on paper because part of me wanted it to be perfect the first time, and that ended up paralyzing me into in-action.

The best advice I can share is to get it started today. Start somewhere. Get something down on paper and begin reading it every day. It could be something as simple and powerful as, I believe in myself. Whatever you decide, just get it in writing and make the conscious effort to read it every day.

Ask yourself, what do I want? What do I value? What do I want to get better at? What kind of person do I want to be? Answer those questions, then write it, say it, feel it, and believe that you are worth it. Trust me, it gets easier in time.

Do you struggle getting up in the morning? Write, and say it with belief, 'I get up each morning with energy and passion.'

Are you struggling to stand up for what you value? Write it, and say it with belief, 'I am unshakable in my values.' Is it hard to look yourself in the mirror? Write it, and say it with passion, 'I am beautiful. I radiate peace, love, and forgiveness.'

Write it, say it, believe it, and be it! There is no right or wrong way, just start somewhere. Customize it to you, and continually sharpen it as you change and grow. I struggled through a large part of my life, beating myself up with my thoughts. At times, I still find myself doing it, but I'm working on it, and it's getting easier.

My thoughts used to be filled with doubt, fear, guilt, and despair. I created habits of talking to myself that way until the negativity became second nature. Addiction preys on those destructive states and uses them to wedge its way in, spreading more seeds of doubt and despair.

So, for me, daily reinforcements are a must. One of the first things I do each morning is read my, "I am…" statement. I use the morning hours to study, pray, and journal my thoughts. For me, the morning just works better. This practice manifests itself throughout the day as I lean on those reinforcing thoughts. Remember, the words you choose to think will create your reality.

The words in my "I am…"statement help me stay the course. Create one that is personal to you, and that will help you stay the course in your endeavor. If it's alright, I am going to share my "I am…"statement with you.

Here is how it reads today...

"I am...

I am a child of God. I am created original like each of our breathtaking sunsets. I shine authentically like each magnificent sunrise. I am blessed with limitless potential. With it, I am thorough, I am confident, and I get things done, making a positive difference in the lives of many. Each day is a gift, a blessing, and an opportunity. I embrace the present moment as such. I serve others with full purpose of heart and I do all things with love. I am blessed with a warrior spirit. I've awakened and am each day strengthening my warrior within. I have on the armor of God and feel the Spirit guiding me in all that I do. Through the peaks and valleys, my heart feels with gratitude. And with resilience I endure valiantly to the end. I am tall, I am strong, I am true. I return with honor. I am of infinite worth. So, with a smile on my face, my eyes full of kindness, and my heart filled with love, I embrace each step along my path, knowing I am serving as a beacon of light.

I am...Ryan David Hiatt."

Have fun as you design your life by deciding the words you choose to direct your journey. Customize it, adapt it, and build upon it as you grow.

Since thoughts are things, **what are you going to do about it?**

30

'Watch your Actions'

"Whatever you do, or dream you can, begin it. Boldness has genius and power and magic in it."

-Johann Van Goethe

I believe, deep down we know what we need to do. Whatever it may be. Things like excelling at work, becoming a better spouse, a better parent, or just an overall better person. Whatever it is, I believe we know what needs to be done. So, why does it seem so difficult to just get up and do it? Why, at times, does it feel so hard to do the things we know will benefit our lives?

"Knowing is not enough, we must apply. Willing is not enough, we must do."

-Johann Von Goethe

The key to our strength lies in our day to day actions. The actions we take, each day, overtime will define who we are.

Sometimes it can feel overwhelming, especially when you begin to understand just how much heartache and pain you've caused all around you. I've felt that way before, as the shame and guilt from my choices piled up inside me.

I think pain can be healthy to an extent if it is used as a catalyst to change, but if it begins to feel like it's bogging you down, remember to be where your feet are, doing all you can in the present moment.

A pinnacle part of my recovery is nurturing harmony between my conscience and myself. I am finding that when my day to day <u>actions</u> are consistent with my values and purpose, the harmony between my conscience and myself is nourished. I begin to feel peace in knowing that, in this moment, I am doing what needs to be done, and what should be done. Helping me be present and avoid getting harrowed up in guilt and shame from the past. The future has a way of taking care of itself and the past has a way of healing itself, if we take care of ourselves in the present moment.

If you are at all like me, over the years you've created habits that yield pain. Initially it will be challenging to replace those habits with actions that are aligned with who you truly want to be, but don't give up. Those actions will build character and that character will bring strength and courage to your Warrior Within.

I had a visit from my son and mom, just a few months after his sixth birthday. I sat behind the glass, listening to my expressive son tell me about his life. I was enthralled as he spoke of his world, relating some of his latest experiences with me.

With so much animation he told me about his school, dance class, and karate class. I looked on through the glass and felt hope as he smiled and laughed with me. My heart hurt for him as I tried to imagine the challenges he must be faced with, because I wasn't there.

As he told me about his experiences in karate class, I remarked, "Cool buddy, you'll be able to practice self-discipline." He immediately stopped what he was saying, cocked his head to the side, and paused for a moment. Then he said something very powerful. He said, "Yeah dad, and self-discipline is doing something without having to be told to do it."

Those wise words, from the mouth of my six-year-old son, brought a profound image to my mind. 'Doing something without having to be told to do it.'

And there I sat, imprisoned, at thirty-one years old, and finally dealing with the consequences from my <u>lack</u> of self-discipline. I'm grateful for the insight and sincerity in my son's word. It sparked a simple clarity to the principles of initiative and action.

I'm learning the importance of exercising them with persistence each day. If our actions compromise with our conscience then those seeds of guilt and negativity are sown, and in time they sprout up like thistle, choking out our dreams.

"What we do on some great occasion will depend on what we are and what we are will be the result of previous years of self-discipline."

-H. P. Liddon

The choice is yours, will your actions compromise with your conscience or will they create harmony between conscience and self? My friend Robert asks himself a question when he's faced with challenges in his recovery, he simply asks, "Do I want to go forward or do I want to go back?" He just reached six years sober. His story gives me hope.

In March of 2012, I decided it was time for a change. I decided to leave my position as coordinator for the treatment program. I held that position for a year, feeling so blessed for the growth it afforded me, but I knew it was time for change. I grew alongside others in there and hope I helped them like they helped me. In a lot of ways, that opportunity saved my life.

The morning after I left the treatment program I had an experience that was in my face and put my resolve to the test.

I started on a work crew and that morning I was offered a chew and a smoke from one of the other inmates. Now, for me, I knew I'd feel guilty if I made that compromise. I would start lying and then I would start this painful cycle all over again. I knew because it happened years ago, and here I sit in prison, partially as result of it.

That choice was staring me right in the face. Would I choose to go forward or would I choose to go back? I began hearing the subtle whispers of my addiction saying, *"What will the other guys think of you, it's only chew, nobody has to know, nobody will ever know, you deserve this, you need this, you need me."*

Thankfully, the Warrior Within me stood firm as I responded, "No thanks, I *don't* chew and I *don't* smoke. I've got enough vices." Simple as that.

It may seem insignificant but turning it down meant everything to me, in that moment. It was hard at first, part of me wanted it, but each time I stood my ground I felt a little bit stronger, until eventually the guys just accepted it as who I was. After a while they came to know that tobacco was just something I didn't do. In a way, I think they respected me for standing for something.

That small action helped me in more ways than you could imagine. I believe it's helping me come from a place of integrity within, especially since I lived a lie for so much of my life. The simple actions of each day matter. There is an ocean of potential within each one of us, and I believe the world needs it now, more than ever. Our families need us, our communities need us, but the question of whether we answer the call to action, is up to us.

"The difference between what we do and are capable of doing would suffice to solve most of the worlds problems."

-Mahatma Ghandi

What do you dream of doing? What do you feel you were born to do? There is no better time than now to act. Goals, visions, hope, faith, and purpose without action are nothing; they're like a mist of unconquerable dreams floating around in the mind, tossed around with the tides of time. The real beauty and strength is in the action. Those simple, day-to-day actions, will shape us and overtime enable us, to reach our vision.

Embrace today as a gift, a blessing, and an opportunity. Find peace in this moment and it will open-up to you and allow you to take fluid action.

"All men dream, but not equally. Those who dream by night in the dusty recesses of their minds wake in the day to find it was vanity. But the dreamers of the day are dangerous men for they may act their dreams with open eyes to make it possible."

-T.E. Lawrence

What can you do today to become a better person? What have you been putting off? What are you neglecting? Listen to your heart, it will guide you.

Maybe it's going for a jog to clear your head and reflect. Maybe it's praying for guidance, or finding some support or advice, maybe it's being honest, coming clean, finding your purpose. Whatever it is, believe in yourself, even if it feels like the hardest thing to do, and act upon it.

There is no better time than right now.   Tomorrow never comes when it comes to making changes. All we ever have is now. By taking it one step at a time, little by little, those steps add up. At times the steps may feel impossible, or the pain you feel may seem unbearable; breakthrough anyway, you can do it. Trust that it all adds up in the end.

Remember, you are of infinite worth.

So, what are you going to <u>do</u> about it?

31

'Watch your Habits'

"We are what we repeatedly do. Excellence, then, is not an act, but a habit."

-Aristotle

Some of the greatest causes of pain in my life can be traced back to a direct reflection of my daily habits. Relapse after relapse, lie after pathetic lie, broken promise after broken promise, again, and again, and again, I always fell back. Although I wanted to change, my habits didn't reflect that desire. So, I'd last a month, or maybe even a few months, but eventually I would always fall back to my old ways, my habits made sure of it.

What I'm learning today is the sheer significance of the habits we choose to ingrain into our daily life. Especially the first few years of recovery. Countless times over the past few years, I've heard the whispers of my addiction, seducing me to fall.

There have been times where I almost fell, but the sheer root of the habits I'm engraining have helped me to stand firm.

I believe that if we are not moving forward then we're moving back. There is no such thing as stagnant time. I must consciously ask myself questions like...

'How can I strengthen my daily routine? How can I strengthen the habits I currently have? What else can I do each day to get me more on track? What habits do I need to replace? Am I moving forward? Am I getting stronger? What else could I be doing?'

The challenging part is sticking with them while they become a habit. Falling into complacency can be just as vicious of a killer as compromise.

"Remember that the most difficult tasks are consummated not by a single explosive burst of energy, but by consistent daily application of the best you have within you."

-Og Mandino
<u>The greatest miracle in the world</u>

Oftentimes, I sit on my bunk, here behind these walls, and think about what my life experience has come to. During all the years of drug abuse I created so many bad habits, they became engrained into my mind, controlling the way I thought.

At times, the mountain in front of me seems impossible. I hear the whispers of my mind telling me to give up, again. But, just as I have engrained those bad habits, I can reprogram my mind to think differently. I can engrain habits rooted in faith, integrity, persistence, passion, initiative, discipline, and honor.

One step at a time, as we create healthy habits and consistently build upon them, they become etched and ingrained into our character. Becoming part of us, a reflection.

By nurturing our thoughts and acting upon them, the soul will begin to shine brighter. As you climb the mountain before you, it may feel like you aren't getting anywhere at all or that it's no use even trying, each step matters, even if you or no one notices, it matters. So, keep at it.

I'm here to tell you that one day soon you'll be blessed with one of those sacred moments of peace and clarity, the light will shine from behind those storm clouds and bring warmth to your soul.

The light will illuminate the path, allowing you to glimpse all that you have endured, and you'll see it is beyond worth it. Every step matters, you are gaining ground, and you'll discover the faith within to press on, one beautiful step at a time.

"As a single footstep will not make a pathway in the earth, so a single thought will not make a pathway in the mind. To make a deep physical path we walk again and again. To make a deep mental path we must think over and over the thoughts we wish to dominate our lives."
-Henry David Thoreau

There will be days when you feel discouraged, especially thinking about all the pain and damage caused in addiction, but I encourage you to be where your feet are, take another step, and remember to breathe. Those are the days it's most important to fall back on the habits you've been engraining into your character.

Our habits begin in our thoughts, in the way we choose to think of ourselves, our future, and our possibilities. Those thoughts create our actions, and with faith, courage, determination, and continuous effort we can engrain the habits we wish to dominate our lives.

So, what do you want out of life? What do you value in this life? What do you want to be remembered for?

Align those thoughts with actions, those actions will forge habits that will take you along the ride that is your life!

Our habits can lead us to dance with the stars, or they will lead us to drown in misery and pain.

So, what are you going to do about it?

32

'Watch your Character'

"Character is the quality that embodies many important traits such as integrity, courage, perseverance, confidence, and wisdom. Unlike your fingerprints that you were born with and can't change, character is something that you create within yourself and must take responsibility for changing."

-Jim Rohn

Embodied in the miracle of recovery, is that intangible thing called character. Character is a silent force that carries us along our path, rooted firmly behind every step, every choice, every desire, and every decision. I believe character is visible in the eyes, for all to see, a reflection of the soul.

I am grateful for the challenge from Jim Rohn, that we must take responsibility for changing our character. I believe it is of utmost importance. Though character can be visible in the eyes for all to see, I believe there are times when it must be revealed to ourselves personally. Showcasing to ourselves just who we are and what we are made of.

We reach a point where, due to the obstacles and trials made in our lives, we must reveal to ourselves who we are as we triumph over adversity. I believe those moments can come in our darkest hours, amidst those beautiful moments of adversity and challenge.

As sure as the sun still rises, the storms of life will undoubtedly come, possibly even more so when we choose to make a change. But one thing I'm learning, is that with each purposeful step we take, or each time we stand tall amidst the struggles, our character is being shaped, tested, and proven. It will, in-turn, strengthen who we are, so that when adversity comes again we are pre-disposed to embrace it as our ally. Allowing us the faith and persistence to stand firm.

Embodied in the power of change is the character that has been forged in the refiners' fire, quenched by the tears, and hammered and forged again, and again.

I believe recovery is more than just staying clean and sober, it is an awaking to one's purpose, a choice to live well by finally realizing the ocean of potential one has within; an awakening of the authentic self. Character can serve as the vessel that carries us home.

When I think about what the future holds for me and what kind of challenges are next for me, along my path, I am reminded of just how important it is to continually strengthen my character; a direct reflection of my thoughts, actions, and habits.

Will I be strong enough to stand up for what I know in my heart is right? Will I choose to stand tall? Especially when no one seems to care, or when no one is looking?

There will be tests, some big, some may seem small, but they all matter and the choice is so preciously yours. While in these cradles of adversity some obstacles may be of your own making and others might not, but whatever the challenge may be, embrace it, and grow from it.

"What would the world look like if everyone did what you did?"

Would the world be a better place? That question helps me consider my actions and gauge my own character. It's clear to me that I have a lot of work to do.

For so many years I caused chaos and discontent in the world, I'm grateful today for the opportunity to build the new.

As we near the end of this book, I want to share the thing I believe is of most importance. Thank you for bearing with me. Because at the end of the day, we're just people trying to find a better way, and I'm learning that it was never fully in our hands anyway.

I believe, after we've done all we can do, there comes a time when we realize that the best tools man can produce just aren't enough. After trying on my own and failing, time and time again, I finally reached a pinnacle point of surrender, realizing I could not do it on my own anymore.

It was finally time to put faith over fear.

"People are often unreasonable and self-centered,
forgive them anyway.
If you are kind, people may accuse you of ulterior motives.
Be kind anyway.
If you are honest, people may cheat you.
Be honest anyway.
If you find happiness, people may be jealous.
Be happy anyway.
The good you do may be forgotten tomorrow.
Do good anyway.
Give the world the best you have and it may never be enough.
Give your best anyway.
For you see, in the end it is between you and God.
It was never between you and them anyway."

-Mother Theresa

33

'Have a Little Faith'

For me, I tried and failed, time and time again. No matter how hard I tried, no matter how bad I wanted it, I came up short, every single time. Desperately I wanted to stop the pain and stop shattering the hearts of all those around me. I wanted to break free from the shackles and chains of my addictions, but no matter how bad I wanted it, I fell short every single time.

What was I missing? Why, no matter how hard I tried, did I always end up falling back?

A stubborn resistance inside me kept pulling me down. No matter how hard I tried, I was unable to bend the world around me to my will. Until finally, the pain, frustration, and hopelessness I felt, humbled me to my knees.

I was so tired and worn from the battle I was fighting. I reached a point where I realized I couldn't do it alone anymore. So, I prayed to my God with all my heart from that prison cell. In the comfort of my soul I felt two distinct feelings; the understanding that I couldn't do it alone, and an all-encompassing peace and comfort in knowing that *I am not alone.*

"Work as though everything depends on you, pray as though everything depends on God."

-Saint Augustine

The relationship between us and God is intimately personal. I believe in a God of miracles, who loves me, and guides my feet. I also had to go through hell to find faith, and for that I am so grateful today.

The foundation of my recovery must be planted firmly on faith in God. For me, Paramount to any of the practices outlined in this book, is the importance, of keeping in constant contact with God through prayer.

Whoever you are, wherever you are, and whatever you are up against, you can choose to pray. Right now if you want, and that is a beautiful thing.

I believe it is our responsibility as individuals to build and strengthen that precious relationship. I also believe it is something so sacred and personal, that one must seek, search, trust, and experience it for oneself. The only thing I can say is,

Have a little faith.

I don't know much, but one thing I do know is that prayer is a powerful thing, one of the best of things, especially for an addict like me.

Whether you're on a riverbank and experiencing a moment of peace, or you're on the street corner momentarily stopped by the magnificence of the setting sun; you can pray. Maybe you're looking up at a billion stars as they light up the night sky, and you're feeling so small, yet so infinitely special; you can pray.

Or maybe you're kneeling on the concrete floor of your jail cell, while your eyes can't hold back the tears from your soul any longer, whoever you are and wherever you are, you can choose to pray.

"Prayer is not asking, it is a longing of the soul, it is an admission of one's weakness. And so, it is better in prayer to have a heart without words than words without heart."
-Mahatma Ghandi

Through the power of prayer, I can embrace each step with trust and faith, no matter how hard some steps may be. With <u>faith,</u> I believe I can do what I know in my heart to be right. With <u>faith,</u> I believe I can live the life I know I was designed to live. With <u>faith,</u> I can live a life free from the shackles and chains of my addictions.

There will be times when I feel I just can't go on another step, or when I feel as if the mountain in front of me is too daunting to bear; but at the core of my belief I know that I am not alone. That faith gets me through.

I believe in a loving God who wants what's best for me. Seek, search, and find your God. Find your truth. There is no corner too dark, and no pit too deep, for the healing light of God's love.

I feel indebted to Him who carries me and who made the ultimate and infinite sacrifice for me. I feel a calling and a duty burning deep within me to serve Him.

There is so much good that can be done in our world. I personally believe that it all starts with becoming the person we are designed to be, which enables us to be able to give our best. Even a kind word, a smile, or a good example will branch from the family, to our communities, and to the world we live in.

"The only certain means of success is to render more and better service than is expected of you, no matter what your task may be. This is a habit followed by all successful people since the beginning of time. Therefore, I say, the surest way to doom yourself is to perform the minimum of what is required."
-Neal A. Maxwell

There is no telling what is next on the journey or who will cross your path. I am learning the key is to be continually preparing. If we open our eyes I'm sure we can find something we can do for someone each day. There is so much good that can be done in this world and, if you're an addict in recovery, I believe your words carry more weight to the addict who still suffers, because they know you've walked down some of those same dark streets.

By getting up, getting involved, and giving back, we can make a difference, and I believe we can stay the course. Find your plan and work it like your life depends on it.

In the rooms of recovery, I'm finding strength, experience, support, and hope. I strongly encourage you to find fellowship in a twelve-step program. Whatever you need there is a fellowship waiting with open arms. I'm working the steps, they help me, I believe they can help you, and through that you can help others.

Your light is something personal and unique, only you have your light, and your light will help shine light to others. Darkness cannot cover light, so light up the darkness!

I believe each of us has a Warrior Within, standing guard, and urging us along our eternal destiny. No matter who you are, what challenges you face, or what mistakes you've made along your path, you have within you the gift and ability to shape what you are becoming; to shape your being.

As I sit here on my bunk, writing the final words in this book, I remain hopeful for what's next along the road of life. Doubts and fears try and sink their claws into me, the opposing force will always be there, waiting in the shadows and trying new tricks to seduce me off the path, but I can be grateful for this trial. It brought me to my knees, helped me have the willingness to surrender to a better way of life, and helped me trust and understand that darkness cannot cover light.

Those enticing whispers of the opposing force will always be there in the shadows of my mind; the key is not too listen to them.

My hope and my prayer is that I can have the willingness to continue listening to my heart, my soul, and the Warrior I have Within me.

My problems with addiction aren't unique. It's happening all around us. I'm just a guy who made some stupid decisions and lost his way. I am grateful for a new shot at life. I am grateful to be experiencing a change in my heart. I am grateful for a loving God, a forgiving God, and the infinite sacrifice that made forgiveness possible.

Thank you for letting me share my experience with you. As I wrote this book I've been inspired every step of the way. I couldn't have done it without God's comfort, guidance, and love, which eases my burdens, lifts me up, and urges me forward.

I've prayed and felt Him wipe away my tears and fill my heart with love. As I come to the close of this book I anxiously look forward to the next chapters of my life. I know there will be challenges ahead, but my heart is filled with a new freedom and a new hope.

I'm excited to hold my son again, I'm excited for him to have his daddy back. I'm excited about the life ahead of me and I am grateful for what this trial is teaching me.

My heart is full of so much gratitude today. I wish you Godspeed along your journey. Whoever you are, whatever you are faced with in this life, no matter how dark the field around you is or how lost you feel you are, I leave you with one last thought, one truth, and one love.

> *"The future is as bright as your faith."*
> *-Thomas S. Monson*

And I ask...

Have You Had Enough?

EPILOGUE

It's July of 2017, the warm winds of the season are cooled by a summer rainstorm. I'm sitting here, in the comfort of my home, preparing to publish the book I wrote in prison.

A multitude of miracles have happened in my life since those years I spent in a cell. I was released from prison on January 6th, 2015. I walked into the loving arms of my son that day, a hug I will always remember. Tears streamed down my face as I held family in my arms, knowing that I stayed the course while I was in there.

The bright lights of the real world brought with them new challenges, but I was blessed with the faith and the willingness to keep pressing forward, one day at a time.

I enrolled into school and began studying things that would help me along my path of purpose. My family showed up for me in a way that I am beyond grateful for. I am a living, breathing testimony that relationships heal, the past doesn't have to be our identity, and recovery is possible. I am learning today to trust my healing.

I remember the day I was finally released from parole. It was a day I had waited my whole adult life to experience, and it was finally happening. I got into my car and headed south, stopping by to visit the officers at the jail and some great friends from Beaver, Utah. These heroes believed in me and treated me like a human being when I was caged behind those walls. I am eternally grateful for them. I left there and headed straight for the beach in California.

I sat on that beach all day long as the tears from my eyes fell into the salt of the ocean as I poured my heart out in gratitude to my God, for blessing me with a new freedom, and a life I only dreamed of.

Today I am involved in a twelve-step fellowship, it helps me stay grounded and remember what got me here. I am blessed with opportunities to share my story with people who are struggling with the battle within. I feel a calling within me to help bring light to those who feel only darkness.

I was blessed with the opportunity to marry the soul of my dreams. On the most perfect day, on the sandy shores of Crescent Bay Beach, we held each other's hand, looked through the tears of love in each other's eyes...knowing we had finally made it home. We remembered.

Gods timing is perfect and I am so grateful today for the life I am blessed with. As I write these words today my eyes are covered in tears, my heart is full of hope, and I believe in love.

Recovery is worth it, you are worth it, and there is no corner too dark for the light of Gods love.

Today I have been clean and sober for 2,276 days. I picked up my six-year medallion a few months ago, Dominic asked me, "Hey dad, did you get your sober chip?" When I told him yes he said, "Oh, great dad. I am so glad you're sober. I sure love you." That right there was worth all the pain.

I'm working on my next book, and this one is filled with hope. Forever grateful, one day at a time.

Feel free to follow my blog at:

www.HaveIHadEnough.com

Or on Instagram at:

@i.am.authentically.me

My incredible wife puts her heart and soul into her work at the *American Foundation for Suicide Prevention*. If you, or someone you know is struggling with mental illness please go to:
www.afsp.org
They are the nation's leading private funder for research into suicide prevention. Please stay. Find out how you can get involved and, *Be the Voice*.

With Love and Light.

89572913R00115

Made in the USA
San Bernardino, CA
27 September 2018